RAUCOUS ADVENTURES

OF AN

ALASKAN TRAMP LOGGER

LAWRENCE DAVIS

National Library of Canada Cataloguing in Publication

Davis, Lawrence D., 1930-
     Raucous adventures of an Alaskan tramp logger /
Lawrence D. Davis.

ISBN 1-4120-0792-5
     I. Title.

SD537.52.D38A3 2003   634.9'8'092   C2003-904163-8

TRAFFORD

This book was published *on-demand* in cooperation with Trafford Publishing. On-demand publishing is a unique process and service of making a book available for retail sale to the public taking advantage of on-demand manufacturing and Internet marketing. **On-demand publishing** includes promotions, retail sales, manufacturing, order fulfilment, accounting and collecting royalties on behalf of the author.

Suite 6E, 2333 Government St., Victoria, B.C. V8T 4P4, CANADA

Phone	250-383-6864	Toll-free	1-888-232-4444 (Canada & US)
Fax	250-383-6804	E-mail	sales@trafford.com
Web site	www.trafford.com	TRAFFORD PUBLISHING IS A DIVISION OF TRAFFORD HOLDINGS LTD.	
Trafford Catalogue #03-1160		www.trafford.com/robots/03-1160.html	

10   9   8   7   6   5   4   3   2   1

ACKNOWLEDGEMENTS

I owe a very special thanks to:

Family members, friends, and especially my creative writing instructor and classmates, who encouraged me to write this book.

The Swede for recalling incidents I had forgotten.

My loving companion for transcribing my scribbled stories, typing, editing, retyping many drafts, formatting and finalizing the book for publication.

Jean Bucknum, for her technical expertise and assistance in enhancing the photos/sketches and scanning them into the book.

Lloyd and Ellen Keeland, co-authors of the book "Loon Lake Lloyd", for their advice and helpfulness.

Kathleen Olsson who designed the cover and provided many illustrations for the book.

INTRODUCTION

This is a rather offbeat book of the years I spent as a tramp logger in Alaska during the 1960's. My remembrances include events that were often dangerous and life threatening; many ribald adventures while on R & R (rest and relaxation) from the logging camps; and humorous tales of antics of bears and other native Alaskan wildlife I had the good fortune to witness. I've attempted to relay these tales with humor whenever possible.

It's time to straighten out a misconception that most loggers are lumberjacks. As I understand the term, lumberjack meant that you rode rafts of logs down rivers a long time ago in Wisconsin and Michigan. I do know that most loggers don't like being called lumberjacks.

Tramp loggers are hard workers in an extremely dangerous occupation. They worked in very secluded logging camps, often accessible only by small planes. They usually worked from dawn to dusk, seven days a week, and stayed in camp for months on end until a major holiday like the Fourth of July, when the logging show shut down for maintenance. That would give the loggers the opportunity to fly into town for at least four or five days of heavy-duty party time. A logger can build up a good chunk of money in the two months or so he is in camp, a lot of restless energy after gambling with his life every day, and in most cases, great gobs of stupidity.

You ask what does a tramp logger do when he hits town with a pocket full of money? He drinks and fights. My personal preference was the bars with dance floors because you had more room to maneuver while delving into the finer arts of fisticuffs.

Most loggers, tramp or not, have marched to a different drummer all their lives. Most of them have been put in an "I don't give a damn" state by some disaster in life, be it divorce, the death of someone near and dear, bankruptcy, or other emotional traumas. This may be why loggers seem to have more tolerance to physical pain than the average white-collar worker. When a limb, a log, or well-thrown punch knocks them done, it's something to laugh about the next day. However, if you humiliate one of the tramp loggers, you best be looking over your shoulder for a long while.

I don't mean to imply that all loggers who worked for months on end in secluded logging camps were wild and boisterous during camp shut downs. Many were devoted family men who either remained in camp during shut-down periods or flew home to visit their wives and loved ones. In fact, some of the fly-in camps had separate facilities available for loggers who wished to bring their families out to stay with them at the site.

TABLE OF CONTENTS

CHAPTER I

A New Beginning - North to Alaska

In the early 1960's, I decided the best way to get over my divorce was to get the hell out of Oregon. The question was "Where to go?" My destination was decided when I met the Swede, a friend of my Dad. The Swede told me he was planning to head for Alaska in about two weeks to work in the woods. That sounded like a great idea, so I gave a two-week notice at my job and got ready to go.

I had a friend in Prince Rupert, British Columbia, so we decided to drive up, leave my car there and take the ferry from there to Juneau. My love affair with Alaska was about to begin. We left Reedsport about nine in the morning, me with all my rigging, the Swede with all of his gear plus his pint of whiskey. We were going to share the driving, but after he finished his whiskey, I knew that wasn't going to happen.

We arrived at the Canadian border after dark. I told my drunken companion to stay in the car and let me do all the talking. I went into the customs office and was doing the paperwork when in staggered the Swede. He wandered over to the customs agent and boisterously challenged him to an arm wrestling match. The agent declined, but the Swede was loudly insistent.

Naturally that didn't go over too well with the agent in charge who proceeded to strongly advise me to get the Swede back in the car and out of Canada immediately. The Swede wasn't very happy with that directive and proceeded to tell him, "We're going to cross the border whether you like it or not."

The agent told him he couldn't get two miles over the border before the Royal Canadian Mounted Police would stop him. My companion's answer was "Good, I've always wanted to kick a Mounties's ass."

The agent's response was, "I used to be a Mountie."

I could see things were going downhill fast and was trying to drag the Swede back to the car. The ex-Mounties's last words were, "Get him the hell out of here fast, or neither one of you will ever cross this border."

The Swede's parting words were, "I always knew you Canadians were chicken shit." I finally got the Swede back into the car, and we headed back to Blaine, Washington, to spend the night.

The next morning my traveling companion was sick, sober and sorry. There was one added plus though; he was very quiet. We sailed across the border with no problems on our way to the next adventure.

I drove all the way to Prince George, B.C., the next day traveling up the beautiful Frazier River Highway. The mountains were still wearing their winter caps of white. The river was rushing through the deep gorges in a frantic rush to get to God only knows where.

2

We rented a motel that night in Prince George. Naturally, we felt we had to sample the town's social life, and went to a nearby bar. We were surprised to see three separate connecting rooms to the bar, each with its own entrance. One partitioned area was for men only, another was for women only, and the middle section was for couples only.

The Swede and I went into the men's side. He proceeded to get into a shuffle board game with some of the locals and won about $100. Of course, that didn't go over too well with the regulars and came close to ending up in a fight. However, cooler heads prevailed, and the Swede came over and sat with me at the bar.

He pointed to a poster hanging on the barroom wall picturing what was apparently a prostitute. Under the picture was a warning that one out of three had some form of venereal disease. The Swede laughed and said, "Hell, that's not bad odds."

The Swede got busy plotting against the three-door system. He decided the best way was to go back outside, snag one of the cuties standing around the bar entrance, and come back into the bar together. I was tired after driving all day and decided I needed rest more than romance so I retired to the motel.

I don't remember if my companion scored or not, but do remember him coming in late as hell and being very unhappy about someone stealing his coat. He kept saying he was going to kick the shit out of any Indian he saw the next day because he was sure it had been an Indian that had taken his coat.

We continued on our trip the next day and arrived in Prince Rupert in the early afternoon without any more incidents. We visited with my friends for the next two days and then boarded a ferry bound for Juneau. The approximate 550-mile journey by ferry would last four days and three nights.

It was too early in the season for tourists, so very few passengers were on the ferry. Fortunately, this gave us a choice of either renting a room on board or sleeping on huge padded couches in the nearly vacant viewing area. Being cheap and wanting to save our money for party time, we decided we could travel in comfort on the padded benches.

I became acquainted with an Alaskan native on the ship, who I think was a Tlingit Indian. We talked for quite some time while he told me many of his native customs and beliefs. We were standing on the bow of the ship when we spotted a pod of killer whales. This was fascinating to me so I was very interested in watching them.

Suddenly the native grabbed me by the arm and turned me around to face away from the whales. He told me he believed that watching the whales would bring bad luck, and he didn't want his new friend to have any bad luck either.

4

The ferry ran into a severe storm with bitter cold weather that encased the ship in a layer of ice. That forced us to spend the last day and night of the ferry trip in the heated viewing area. We finally arrived at our destination, beautiful Juneau, Alaska.

Arrival at Juneau

When I say beautiful, I mean breathtakingly beautiful. As soon as you step off the ferry, you're greeted by the sight of lush green, heavily forested, snow-capped mountains that reach almost to the edge of the water. There is barely room enough for the one street that runs between the deep port of the Gastineau Channel and the Pacific Coast Mountain range that borders Juneau and British Columbia.

The side of the street next to the water has a large sprawling cold-storage plant for processing fish. On that same side of the street is a series of bars, liquor stores, and one café. On the opposite side you'll find the Franklin, a hotel, which was dug out and built into the side of the mountain. Steep wooden stairs, sometimes three or more flights, lead up to several apartment houses.

About half way up the mountain across the street from the ferry terminal, and, if you know where to look, is the entrance to the Joe Juneau mine. I'm ashamed to admit I've never been inside the mine, but understand there are miles of tunnels reaching deep inside the mountain. I also heard that great gobs of that pretty yellow metal called gold was once extracted from the mine.

The waterfront is known as the bad part of town. Needless to say, I got to know it well. The rest of the city is scattered with grocery stores, churches, private homes, better hotels and the State Capitol office buildings. There are a few elite bars in the better part of town where the State representatives can gather and discuss how they can piss away the taxpayer's money while sipping on their high dollar drinks.

Here's a little historical background on Juneau. Juneau was the capitol of the Alaskan Territory when its citizens erected a large five-story capitol building in 1931. When Alaska became the 49th state in 1959, Juneau remained as capitol city using the existing capitol building.

For those of you who do not already know, Alaska is the largest state in the union, more than twice as big as Texas, and is one-fifth as large as the rest of the United States.

Juneau is a most unusual location for a state capitol as it can only be reached by air or water. There are no tie-in roads connecting Juneau to the rest of the state. However, there is a short road that leads to a fishing town named Auke Bay; a bridge that crosses a fiord to Douglas; and a highway that leads to the airport and Lemon Creek where the jail is located. No, I was never lodged there.

At the end of the highway is the 1¾ mile wide Mendenhall Glacier. I'm not great with descriptive phrases, but from the road at the bottom of the glacier all the way up the snow covered ice, which stretches as far as the eye can see, the exposed ice is the most heavenly blue. You would have to see it to fully appreciate it. In fact, the vastness of the entire state of Alaska makes a person feel as insignificant as an ant in the middle of the Gobi desert.

The Swede and I finally got off the ferry in beautiful downtown Juneau where a whole new chapter of my life was about to begin. It was early spring, too early in fact. Juneau had a very snowy winter that year, and spring was later than usual. We had planned to hire out to work on a logging show when we got there, but four feet of snow still lay on the ground. So we hung around Juneau drinking and, in my case, getting to know the people.

I soon found out that Alaskans are a breed all their own. They were tough but trusting and fun loving. The toughness part was easy to see. If you raised too much hell in one of the bars, did they call the cops? No way! The bartenders would jump over the bar, slap the troublemaker around and throw him out.

If one of the patrons got too drunk and passed out at the bar, the bartender would carry him to a booth in the back to let the over-trained customer sleep it off. As soon as the sleeper could make it back to the bar, the barkeep would start serving him drinks again. If you were able to make it to the sidewalk before passing out, the police would just pick you up and take you home.

The bars opened at 7:00 a.m. and closed the following morning at 5:00 a.m. giving the crew barely time enough to sweep out the place and restock the bar supplies. A person had to be in tip-top shape to put in a full shift in any bar in Juneau or in any other bar in southeastern Alaska at that time.

An acquaintance from Reedsport went to Ketchikan to go to work in the woods. Naturally he had to stop at the first bar he could find. The bartender was one big, ugly and mean dude. The would-be logger, thinking he was hysterically funny, reached over the bar, and pinched the big, mean, ugly bartender on the cheek saying, "God, you're cute."

Before the comedian knew what happened, the barkeep was over the bar, grabbing him by the back of the neck and the seat of his pants. The bartender proceeded to fire him out the door, wrapping him around a parking meter. Besides bruising Mister Logger's hip, the roust broke the would-be comedian's leg.

The bar owner paid the logger's doctor bill and his plane fare back to Reedsport. From what I understand, my Reedsport acquaintance had all of Alaska he could stand and decided never to return.

Now, back to Juneau. My friend, the Swede, had made the same mistake the previous year by getting there too early in the season. Knowing the ropes, according to him, he really hit hard times. The story goes that he did everything he could to stay afloat until the woods opened up. In his word, "Hell, L.D., I even tried pimping, but the damn girls kept sandbagging on me."

Some of his ramblings would send me into gales of laughter. I think the funniest one was, "You know, L.D., I've tried everything but taking drugs or turning gay. You know I'm afraid to try either one because I might like it."

The truth of the matter is that you have to take stories that logging partners tell one another with a grain of salt. Had I told the Swede the same story, it would have gone like this: "Yeah, Swede, I had a damn hard time making ends meet. Hell, a few times I had to rent my beautiful body out to a 65-year-old woman just to stay afloat. The bad part was that I sure didn't make much money as you know how short of cash all ladies on Social Security tend to be."

Everything has to be funny when you are in a high-risk job, especially when any job could be your last. If not, you might have to take a steady job as a "sliver picker" which means, if you don't already know, is go to work in a sawmill.

I think I should explain my relationship with the Swede. My Dad and the Swede's mother dated for several years. Although I was a few years older than the Swede, he took me under his wing to learn the hard cruel facts of high-lead logging. He was like a big brother, a protector, a teacher and a damn good friend.

I didn't need his help in the drinking and raising hell, as I was well past the amateur stage when I met the Swede. I've tried to convince his wife on several occasions, that all our hell-raising in Alaska had been the Swede's fault, and I was as pure as the driven snow when I met him. Not true! I don't think she believed me anyway.

There was another logger who thought he was tough, but actually couldn't lick his lips. He told his girlfriend in a fit of rage that he would hit her so hard the birds would build a nest in her hair before she came to. However, the threat didn't seem to impress or scare her very much.

Here comes the trusting part. When you're not working and having lots of free time, it doesn't take long to run out of money. I had some money in the bank in Phoenix, Oregon, and desperately needed it as soon as possible.

I went to one of the banks in Alaska and told a cashier of my dilemma. She sent me to the manager to retell my sad story. After repeating the story, I told the manager that I realized he would have to phone the bank in Oregon offering to pay for the long distance call.

The elderly manager looked me up and down and said, "Listen, sonny, if you've got guts enough to write a check, I've got guts enough to cash it." He cashed my check, gave me the money, and sent me on my way. Try that in Oregon, or any other state outside Alaska.

It didn't take long for the Swede and me to blow my stake. There was still no work in town. Each day we went to the local hiring hall, the Imperial Bar, looking for any type of logging job anywhere.

I went in on a Friday morning, when Bob, the owner of the bar, told me the Mad Hungarian in Wrangell, needed two hands. This piece of information forced the Swede and me to confess we were dead broke.

Bob said, "Oh, hell, I'll give him a call and recommend both you fools for the jobs." Bob got the owner of the company on the horn and talked with him for some time.

After he finished the conversation, Bob said, "You're hired. There will be plane tickets waiting at the airport for both of you at 2 p.m. today. The Mad Hungarian will meet the plane and fix you up with a place to stay and a place to eat until your first paycheck."

It was just like money from home. Big Dick, the owner of the company, met us at the airport and took us to our lodgings. Seeing it was Friday, he gave each of us $50 walking-around money. He told us that he would pick us up Monday morning at 7 a.m., and we were to make damn sure we were ready to go to work. I knew all this seemed too good to be true and there had to be a catch. We would soon find out what it was.

CHAPTER II

Wrangell - High-Lead Logging Show

Wrangell is a small fishing town southeast of Juneau between Sitka and Ketchikan. The town abuts the Inside Passage and is located almost at the southern tip of Alaska. During the summer months, the town is more or less a tourist trap.

The town is a very scenic area and has become a popular stopover for Alaskan cruise lines. There are a few gift shops, quite a few bars, a grocery store or two, two or three churches, a hotel and a sawmill.

The company crummy picked up the Swede and me at 7 a.m. the following Monday morning. Both of us were ready and raring to go to work. The job was what is called a high-lead logging show. This means that instead of dragging the logs to the landing with cats, the logging was done using a "spar tree," because the terrain is so steep and inaccessible to cats.

The spar tree is a rigged tall stout tree, sometimes as tall as 180 feet that becomes the center of the new landing. I don't mean to bore you with a lot of details, but feel that in order for many readers to better understand some of my experiences, I need to explain a high-lead logging show.

13

High-lead logging tower and equipment

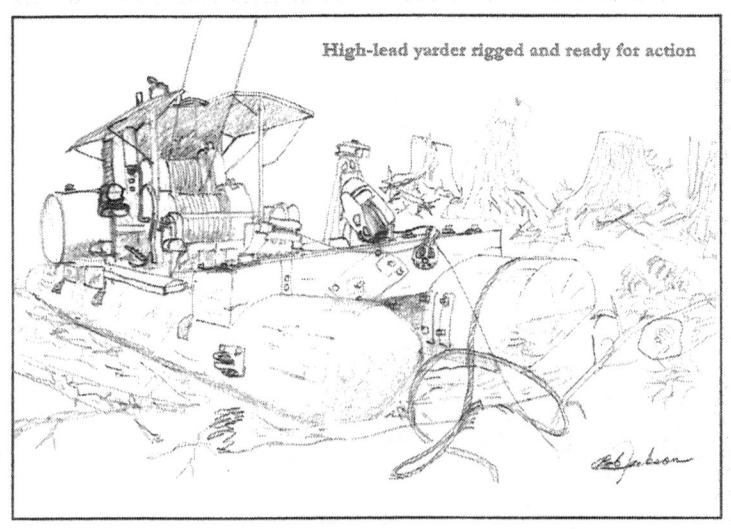

High-lead yarder rigged and ready for action

High-lead
logging show

High climber getting ready to top an old growth tree for use as a spar tree

Cat logging with arch

Yarder engineer hard at work

I'll try to explain high-lead logging in two languages. First of all is the logger terminology. This is being done so I don't piss off seasoned loggers and get called a complete greenhorn. This may still happen as some of the terms have slipped my mind over the years. My excuse is the number of years since I logged coupled with old age. The other is in terms that farmers and laymen hopefully will understand better.

The illustrations and photographs on the previous pages will give you a better concept of some of the terminology used.

The spar tree is always near the top of a hill. It can be a tall stout standing tree or one that is cut and hauled onto the site and raised in place. A logger has to trim off all the branches, cut off the top of the tree, climb to the top and rig the tree.

The spar tree has guy lines going to the top and secured usually to big stumps in all directions so it can stand under the intense stress it will have against it.

The first step, in logger's language, a block, or in layman's language, a pulley, is taken to the top of the spar tree. The tree climber secures the block, and a small cable (called a haywire) is run through the block, back to the ground and onto the yarder.

A yarder is a large machine mounted on skids consisting of two huge drums for the lines of cable to haul in the logs. One is the mainline, the other the haulback, and a small drum for the haywire. The equipment is powered by one, sometimes two diesel engines.

There are several different names for an operator of this machine. I chose to call him a yarder engineer or a donkey puncher.

The following offers more details on the rigging of the spar tree. The climber climbs to the top of the spar tree when the bull block, which I estimate to weigh in at about 1,000 pounds, is pulled to the top by using the yarder and the haywire. The climber secures the bull block.

Then a smaller block called the haulback block is set up and secured. Now the rigging slinger and the choker setter go to work. The tailblock is dragged to the other end of the show, usually by brute force and stupidity.

Now, we have to find a big solid stump to use for the tailhold. Usually two tailholds are used so they can be interchanged so they can cover more area. The tailblock is secured to the tailhold by a huge cable called a rigging strap.

I have to apologize as I've already written several paragraphs of explanations and still haven't gotten one damn log to the landing.

Now the peons, choker setters, really go to work. They have to drag the haywire from the yarder to the tailblock, and then back to the yarder. Not as easy as it sounds. Usually the terrain is as steep as a cow's face, otherwise it would be cat logged.

The choker setters had to make sure the lines weren't hung up on a stump, bushes, etc. If it were, when the line was tightened up, you would have what is called a siwash, which means the line would snap taut into a straight line between the tailblock and the spar tree cutting everything in its path in two, including choker setters.

Now, the haywire is hooked to the haulback line that is a two-inch to three-inch wire cable and is brought back around by the yarder. The haulback

line is then hooked to one end of the butt-rigging
which is a bunch of swivel bells to hang the chokers
from.

The next step is to attach the mainline, which is
about an inch thicker than the haulback, to the other
end of the butt-rigging. Now, we're ready to log.

The brake is set on the mainline drum. The
haulback winch is engaged. The butt-rigging is lifted
off the ground as the haulback is tightened. When it
is at the right height, the brake is loosened and light
pressure is kept on the mainline brake until the logs
are reached. Then the butt-rigging is lowered.

The choker setter grabs the chokers, sets
anywhere from two to four chokers on the ends of
logs, and then runs like hell.

Choker setters

The rigging slinger signals the yarder engineer using a series of loud beeps on an electronic device called a talkie-tooter. Each series of beeps gives a different directive to the yarder operator.

The mainline winch is engaged, the haulback line is braked down, and the logs are lifted off the ground. By applying some brake on the haulback, a full ahead on the main line, the logs are dragged to the landing close to the spar tree. The landing chaser unhooks the chokers from the log. This is done over and over all day long.

The first thing I learned as a choker setter was to set the chokers, run until you felt safe, then run another twenty feet. You soon learn lots of things can happen on a high-lead show, all of which are bad.

Danger – Runaway Log

One time when I was about half way up the hill, a log slipped its chokers and headed back down the hill twisting end over end in my direction. A 34-foot log running wild that way covers a great distance in a very short time.

It seemed to me this log had me right in its sights. I would run left, the log would bounce left. If I ran to the right, the log veered to the right. Now I feel I'm making any National League halfback look like someone's grandmother.

I finally gave up and dove behind a big stump. The log hit the stump, bounced over me, and went on its way. I now did what I didn't have time to do while

I was on the run. I said a prayer, thanked God for sparing me and went back to work.

Runaway log

A later experience was even more terrifying. The Swede and I were standing on a big Spruce stump probably bullshitting, while watching the rigging slinger and the yarder engineer fight a log hang-up. The logs were hung up on a stump. Back and forth they went; each time the logs would hang up again. We were probably enjoying their dilemma, as it gave us what the loggers called "ass time".

Each time the logs snagged onto the stump, their next attempt was even harder and more forceful. You could tell the yarder engineer was getting really pissed off by the black smoke rolling out of the stacks of the twin Jimmy diesels. Something was either going to give or break.

The Swede and I were watching the show standing side by side, our heads about a foot apart,

22

when we heard a big swooshing sound as something flew through the air between our heads. One of us said, "What in hell was that?"

Then it dawned on us at the same time. It was the nub from the end of a choker, a piece of lead about two inches around and shaped like a bullet, going faster than the eye could see. Six inches either way and one of us would have been dead. It left both of us speechless, which takes some doing.

Before I started to describe high-lead logging, I left my story line when the Mad Hungarian hired the Swede and me and paid our way to Wrangell. I remember thinking back then that all his favors were too good to be true.

We soon found out there was a catch. The answer was simple. He couldn't keep good loggers for any length of time because of his bad temper. He paid well, had good equipment, but knew nothing about human nature. Any petty thing would set him off. The tirade of yelling, screaming, swearing and belittling would start and go on and on.

I recall an incident when we were raising a spar tree, had it about two thirds of the way up, and one of the guy lines cut its way into the stump we were using to control the spar tree on the way up which put us at a stand still. Up drives the boss man cursing and screaming.

I was just starting the chain saw to cut the wood from around the line, but stopped to listen to his tirade. The gist of the ranting was "You dumb S.O.B.'s, I should run you all off, fire all you stupid bastards and send you all back to town."

When he paused for breath, I said, "You know, Dick, I've been working here almost two months and that's the first good idea you've had. Why in hell don't you do that?" There was a dead silence, followed by gales of laughter from the crew. Now, the boss is really mad.

His face turned a deep shade of purple, and he couldn't say a word. He stopped down the hill, pausing just long enough to fire the landing chaser for no apparent reason. The boss jumped into his pickup. With the motor roaring, dirt and gravel flying in all directions, he headed back to town.

We soon had the spar tree raised and were ready to continue logging. Who should appear on the job again? You guessed it, our glorious owner and leader. Now we were short one hand, the landing chaser who was fired.

The whole crew, especially the choker setters, were all greenhorns. The company had started another "side," in other words another logging operation, in the same area. This necessitated taking the Swede and the more experienced people over to the new site.

Now the big, bad boss had a serious problem. The landing chaser has to know more than a green choker setter, which narrowed down to one person, me. I'm sure Big Dick had a problem swallowing his pride, not to ask but to tell me that I was going to be the new landing chaser.

The conversation went as follows "L.D., you're going to chase the landing." I responded, "Oh yeah." The owner went on to say, "The pay is better, the work easier, and you'll get more hours." My answer, "I know."

He went on to ask, "So you're taking the job?" I replied "No way." "Why not?" asked the owner.

24

My answer was, "Because you're too damn lazy to walk down the hill and back up just to yell at me. That makes me happy as hell."

Dick went on and said, "What if I promise not to yell at you?" I replied, "You won't be able to contain yourself." He responded with his promise not to yell at me. I told him "O.K., but the first time you bellow at me, I'm on my way to town."

During the course of our conversation, he changed color several times, and I could see his jaw muscles tighten up. We both knew that logging season was in full swing, and good loggers were impossible to find as they had already been hired by other companies.

He pulled up in his pickup and started to stomp toward me once or twice with a bulldog look on his face. I'd just yell at him, "I'll go to town." Back to his pickup he would go, muttering under his breath all the way. It sure made me feel great to know how much he liked and appreciated me. Of course, I jest!

Another time the Mad Hungarian had hired an experienced rigging slinger who was really good. After a couple of weeks on the job, the new rigging slinger asked for a raise. I was standing nearby and was tuned in to the conversation.

Big Dick responded, "Why should I give you a raise. You don't know all that much." The rigging slinger quit on the spot and said as he was leaving, "Spill the ink. I'm going back to school."

Another Dangerous Incident

Back to logging. As I said before, there are a lot of things that can happen on a high-lead show, most of them bad. We sailed along uneventfully for days and days with logs being yarded into the landing and loaded onto trucks by the loader to be sent on their journey to town.

Once in town, some of the logs were loaded on ships destined for Japan, but the biggest and best logs were sent to area sawmills. I knew it was too good to last, and I was right.

The rigging slinger we had at the time was tight-line happy. Once again the "donkey puncher" (yarder engineer) and the rigging slinger were fighting a log hang-up.

I kept hearing the talkie tooter signaling for tight line. This meant that the donkey puncher would stand on the haul back brake, and go ahead with the main line which put great gobs of strain on the spar tree, the main line and the haul back.

With that much stress, something has to give, either the logs or the equipment. This time it was the spar tree. I felt the ground start to shake, saw a guy line stump pulled from the ground and knew I was in deep shit. I knew that the 1,000 pound bull block, the heavy rigging, the guy lines, and however much of the spar tree that broke off would be hanging over my head leaving very little room to run.

My faith in God was reawakened. I prayed again hoping He would hear my pleas for help. I heard a big cracking sound as the spar tree broke off about two-thirds of the way up. I soon realized God was occupied by other problems, and if someone was going to save my ass, it best be me.

I made a spectacular swan dive under the log loader as the world around me crashed down. My only protection was my loggers tin hat, and by then the loader above me. When I was sure everything had stopped falling, I climbed out from under the yarder to see if everyone was all right.

The spar tree had fallen away from the yarder and across the boom of the loader. The loader and the whole unit were draped with guy lines, rigging, etc. The loader operator who was white as a sheet climbed down out of his steel cab. I'm sure he had just finished his chat with God too. Maybe that's why God was busy when I called upon Him for help.

Before long, our glorious leader appeared on the scene, turning the air blue with words that even I hadn't heard very often. Of course, the first thing he did was fire the tight-line happy rigging slinger, and then move me back to setting chokers at the other logging operation. I didn't mind that a bit as it reunited me with my partner, the Swede.

Diving under yarder

Wanigan – Floating Cookhouse/Bunkhouse

I have to tell this part of the Wrangell story sometime, so will tell it now. After about a week in Wrangell, the owner decided he had better get the troops out of town. His reasoning was that it took too long to round up the crew in the mornings to go to work.

Somewhere he found a big barge, complete with kitchen, sleeping quarters, and showers. It had all the comforts of home. In fact, it provided many more comforts than some of the small gypo fly-in camps.

A Wanigan

We had just moved into our new floating home when Big Dick hired two new loggers in town. Both of them were drunk as hell when he drove them out to camp. What Big Dick didn't know was that one of them had a jug of booze in their gear.

The next morning Big Dick stopped at camp on his way to the logging site. Both of the new loggers were still drunk, so he fired them and took them back to town. The last thing I heard them say was "Damn, this is the smallest road stake I've ever left a job with, but hell, I hear this is a gunny sack outfit anyway."

Big Dick hired a female cook from town who was a wonderful lady and a great cook. We were tied up in the river about ten miles out of town. The owner had many faults, but being completely stupid wasn't one of them.

He made damn sure none of the crew would be able to make it back to town after the workday was over. This created a problem for him though, as the cook didn't have transportation to and from town. Now the boss man had to make a decision as to which one of his motley crew he could trust with the crummy to haul the cook back and forth to town each day. I don't know why, but he picked me.

Naturally I was happy to oblige as it meant two more hours pay each day. I would get up two hours before the rest of the crew, drive to town, and pick up the cook so she would have time to prepare breakfast.

I would generally help her out by putting things on the "spike table," which is a table with all the ingredients necessary for the loggers to make their own lunches. I have to admit there was a method to my madness because that early morning extra chore gave me first choice of the lunchmeat, cakes, pies, and cookies.

After the loggers made up their lunches, the wonderful goodies were stored in what we called nosebags, mostly brown paper sacks. Torture or maiming was considered too lax a punishment for stealing any goodie from a fellow logger's nosebag.

Another one of my duties as camp driver was that I was to deliver the crew merrymakers to the local bars and make the rounds to pick them up on Sunday evening. Any other trips to town other than the weekend crummy ride necessitated hiring the local taxicab at the logger's own expense.

You ask, "What happened if the loggers had forgotten to save enough money for the cab fare back to the barge?" The taxi cab driver would put the fare on a tab putting the loggers at his mercy when he figured up his fees.

Sunday was the cook's day off so we all had to fend for ourselves. The cook always left the spike table overflowing and the huge refrigerator stuffed with leftovers. Yes, we really suffered and had it tough. Besides, most of the time the only loggers left in camp on weekends were either broke or sick.

The cook was a married lady, and I stress the word lady. She was married to a fisherman in town. Anyone who knew me soon found out I liked to talk, and sometimes even listened. The cook and I spent a lot of time talking together as we drove back and forth to town and while she was making breakfast. She was probably 10 to 15 years older than I, and we talked and laughed about everything, becoming great friends.

When I picked her up in town about a month later, she was really bummed out. I asked her what the problem was. She told me her husband was really ragging on her about her relationship with me. She told me she would probably have to quit even though they needed the money and she loved the job. This made me very pissed off.

I could see it was time for me to put my unlimited powers of diplomacy to work on this problem. I knew which bars her husband drank in so, when I took the troops into town Saturday evening, I went looking for Mr. Shithead. I made the rounds of the bars and talked to his drinking buddies.

I found out that while he was in the bar in his cups, meaning drunk as a waltzing piss-ant, he was talking about the so-called affair between his wife and me. Now I am really hot. His luck ran out, and I found him. Turning my diplomatic power up to max, I confronted him.

I very carefully explained to him that he couldn't insult me as I was pleased that a lady such as his wife would even take the time to talk with me, but he sure as hell was insulting his wife. I went on to tell him that just because he was stupid, gutless and had a cesspool for a mind, it didn't give him the right to spread his lies all over town. I also pointed out that if he had any guts, he would have confronted me instead of spreading his bullshit all over town.

I guess he hadn't had enough to drink to build up his courage, as he didn't have much to say. I roared on and told him, "If I hear one more word about it from anyone, I will kick your dumb ass all over town." I added the fact that "Anyone who knew his wife from camp and had eaten at her table would be happy to take up the slack in case I wasn't in town and do an even better ass-kicking job than I." I knew the Swede would be happy, make that overjoyed, to do it, as his feelings about ladies was the same as the rest of the loggers in camp.

On our next trip from town to camp, the cook asked if I had talked with her husband. I told her we had quite a discussion. She went on to tell me she didn't have to quit the job, and her fisherman husband treated her with more respect. She added, "I don't know what you said and guess I really don't want to know, but whatever it was, it sure worked." Ah, the power of diplomacy.

I think this is a good place to try to defend the tramp logger. The people in town called us timber beasts, drunken animals, uncouth and a danger to society even though some of the town people made their living from our spending. That included of course the bar owners, the town barflies, and even the town whores.

The word around town spread by one of the whores was that tramp loggers were the least desirable as clients as they had the least money, the biggest cranks often referred to as love tools, and the dirtiest underwear she had ever seen. I'm not too sure I fit all three of the categories, but two out of three isn't bad.

Fun is what we're after at any cost. While the people in town are sipping their martinis or sucking down beer or booze, we are working dry. When the average guy in town wants sex, most of the time his wife or lady friend, and even in those days sometimes a boyfriend, would oblige the need.

When the tramp logger would come to town, he would have to compete with other loggers, fishermen and the town folks. Since we would be in town for only three or four days at the most, we didn't have time to mince around. It's right to the chase, full bore ahead, and the devil take the hindmost.

As for how much we drank, I feel if the truth were known, the martini sipper, the booze sucker and the six-pack a day beer drinker, consumed more alcohol in a year's time than any tramp logger. Throw in the fact that most loggers, tramp or not, have marched to a different drummer all their lives. Most of them have been put in a "I don't give a damn" state by some disaster in life be it divorce, death of someone near and dear, bankruptcy, or other emotional trauma.

So if you should happen onto a drunken logger with a big smile on his face and his honey under his arm, don't look down your nose at him. Show compassion for your fellow man. It's good for the soul, and besides if the look is too abrasive, it could also be very hazardous to your health.

Near Disaster

I know – its time to get back to logging again. After being sent back to log with my almost brother, the Swede, I had one more near disaster. I was working directly under the rigging. It was a hot day and I had removed my hard hat and put it on a stump.

For some reason I still don't understand, I reached back to retrieve my hardhat and put it back on my head where it belonged. I was bent over, trying to work a choker under a log. Suddenly, for some unknown reason, the yarder engineer took his foot off the brake causing hundreds of pounds of line and rigging from the sky to drop on me.

My luck held once again. The rigging hit me on
the slope of the hard hat, shattering it and barely
brushing my shoulder. The impact knocked me
about 40 feet down the hill.

The crew rushed down the hill, expecting to find a mangled bleeding body. What they found was a dazed and furious logger who was getting madder by the second. The first words out of my mouth were "I'm going to kill that son-of-a-bitch. I'll beat him to death with my bare hands."

When my head finally cleared, I started up the hill at a full lope, screaming and cussing all the way. I got within fifty feet of the landing when I ran out of horsepower, adrenaline and breath all at the same time.

I could see the yarder engineer watching from the yarder. I sat down, caught my breath, walked back down the hill, and we proceeded to log for the rest of the day.

That evening when we quit for the day, the yarder engineer was all apologies. He couldn't explain what happened, but told me that if I had made it ten more feet up the hill, he was going to run for the crummy and head for town.

I know loggers reading this will say that I was either the luckiest or unluckiest logger who put on a pair of cork boots. They might also think I was the biggest damn liar that every lived. However, my friend the Swede, who lives only 25 miles away in Reedsport, Oregon, will back up my tales all the way.

Fourth of July Holiday – Back to Juneau

The Swede heard through the grapevine that the camp where he'd worked the year before at Saint James Bay was hiring. We made the decision to work at Wrangell until the Fourth of July holiday, and then head back to Juneau. We were more than ready to leave the employment of the Mad Hungarian when July finally arrived. Last, but not least, was an unforgettable event that happened as were ready to leave town.

Whenever a big tourist ship hit town, the city band always greeted it. While the Swede and I waited for the ferry bound for Juneau, a huge tourist liner docked. Down the gangplank poured a group of gray-haired old ladies, some with grandpa and a few with grandkids. That signaled the band to start its march toward the ship, playing some gawd-awful song.

A guy came running out of the hotel dressed in nothing but his shoes, ran to the front of the band waving his arms like he was twirling a baton and proceeded to lead the band toward the ship.

Two or three spoilsports grabbed him, pulled him away from the front of the band and held him for the cops. At that time, the policy of the police was to give the offender walking-around money and put him on the very next ferry out of town. It didn't matter to the police whether the ferry was headed north or south.

I heard on the radio a few days later that the nude "band leader" ended up in Ketchikan and bailed out of a fourth-floor hotel window. Oh well, I guess he felt he'd had his day of glory.

It was definitely time to leave Wrangell and head for bigger and better things. The ferry finally arrived, and it was back to Juneau time. During the July 4th holiday, the ferry is loaded with tourists so chair seats are limited. As it turned out, it was my time to be the intoxicated traveling companion.

The Swede must have been conserving his money and energy for an assault on the bars in Juneau. I took over a chair in the bar, proceeded to drink and tried to impress everyone within earshot with my logging stories.

I must admit I was a sight to behold. I had a full beard, probably needed a haircut, and of course was being loud and obnoxious. No wonder the Swede stayed away from me during our ferry ride to Juneau.

There was a good reason for the full beard. The mosquitoes and other insects are numerous in the Wrangell area. The mosquitoes are huge. One logger friend of mine swore he saw one big enough to stand flatfooted and seduce a turkey.

Then there were the biting flies we called white socks. When they bit you, the bite swelled up like a bee sting. Another logger friend swore that what the white socks did was take a bite out of its victim and then turn around and take a dump in the hole.

There were also the "no-see-ums" (little sand flies) that were mean little bastards. There were black flies and deer flies. You name it, and those biting bastards were there. I found out that when sporting a full beard, the bug dope didn't sweat out as easily as when you were bald faced.

We arrived in Juneau on a Friday afternoon. The festivities had begun and were already in high gear. I stowed my gear behind the bar at the Imperial Bar, planning on thanking the bar owner for his help in getting us the job in Wrangell, and having a drink or two.

My next plan was to go to the hotel to get a room for the holiday weekend, but there was a sudden change of plans. Just as I was about to go hotel hunting, who should appear but a native honey I had dated before my trip to Wrangell.

She plunked down beside me and asked where I was staying. I informed her I was just on my way to find a room. She told me I could stay at her place but there was a problem. My response was "And what is that?" After a moment's hesitation, she told me had a boyfriend at her place, but he didn't drink and wasn't any fun.

After inquiring about his size and toughness, I told her, "No problem. I'll handle it when we get there."

I'd had just enough to drink on the ferry to feel irresistible and was sure by the time we got there that I'd probably be indestructible besides. My thoughts then were, "Oh boy, what a deal! I just got into town and already had a companion and a place to stay."

After partying all night, we went to her place about 3:00 a.m., and, yes, the boyfriend was there. After a short stare down, I announced that if he was waiting for me to leave, it wasn't going to happen. He left. I sure wish that were the end of the story. No way!

I got up sick and sorry about 9:00 a.m., left her sleeping and went to a café for breakfast. Who do you think was there looking sad and forlorn? The boyfriend.

My first thoughts were "If I had to duke it out with this hangover, I'm dead. One good rap along side my noggin and my whole head would explode." I worried for nothing because he just started to cry on my shoulder telling me how much he loved her and wanted to marry her.

This made me feel like a king-sized asshole. I promised him I would leave her alone and went on my way, still feeling guilty. I picked up my gear, got a hotel room, and slept most of the day.

After the long rest, I was ready to really give Juneau hell and went back to the bars. I knew that sooner or later I would run into the Swede. At the same time I tried to stay away from the places my companion of the night before frequented. After thinking it over, I decided the Occidental Bar located on the waterfront would be a great place to start.

I called the Occidental Bar the gymnasium. That's were the action was if you wanted to fight or watch a fight. The best reason was you didn't have to wait very long either. It was where all the low lives hung out, my type of people at the time. I've had several strenuous workouts there.

One incident resulted in my being knocked through the window in the front door onto the sidewalk. I knew I lost that fight because my opponent had been gone for at least five minutes before I could struggle to my feet.

Oh well, you can't win them all. It was a standing joke with the loggers from St. James Bay. They always asked when I got back from town if I'd been to the Occidental to defend my title.

My conduct in the Occidental Bar reminds me of a story I heard a long time ago. A drunk walked into a bar, eyed the crowd and said, "I can whip any man in this bar." Everyone ignored him.

The drunk went on and bragged "I can whip any man in this town." Again everyone ignored him. Then he yelled out "I can whip any man in the whole state." Same result. No reaction from the onlookers. Then he yelled out, "I can whip any man in the whole damn United States." Still no takers.

Finally he declared loudly, "I can whip any man in the entire world." Someone got up and knocked the drunk on his ass.

After a short pause, the drunk managed to grab onto the bar and pulled himself to his feet. He shook his head several times to clear it, and finally said, "I still say I'm a damn good man, I just took in too much territory."

I didn't realize I left a lasting impression in the bars in Juneau until I flew into town ten years later on my way to the Prudhoe Bay pipeline project. I stopped in the Arctic Bar for a drink. The same owner was there. He said "Hi", and turned to his bartender and told him, "Watch this guy. He'll sit there and quietly drink, smiling all the while, but before you know it, all hell breaks loose."

I hate to admit this, but it made me proud. After all, I was good at something even if was just being bad.

The Occidental Bar was also a place to test your skills in the finer art of fisticuffs, not that I was ready for that yet as I hadn't had any liquid courage. I figured it wouldn't hurt to look over the competition while I judged them.

I knew as soon as I opened the door, it was going to be fun time. Three of the four ugly sisters, my names for them, were sitting there perched on their bar stools. During my short stay in Juneau before the Wrangell job, I'd had many verbal confrontations with the group.

First in line at the bar was Miss America, the one a friend of mine had traded to a boatload of fishermen for a 60-pound King Salmon. After we had a barbequed salmon feast, he took her back. Why? I don't know unless it was for future trades.

Sitting next to her was Hard-Faced Marge, so called because it looked like she put on her makeup with a putty knife. She never had much to say. I always thought she was afraid her makeup would crack.

Third in line was Bashful Betty. She could run through your ancestry in words that even a logger wouldn't use in public.

The fourth ugly sister, Sweet Rose, wasn't there. She probably had a long, hard night. She wasn't much fun to tease anyway. The only reason I brought her up is because the Swede said she looked like a goldfish. After taking a closer look, I decided he was right.

No, they weren't sisters, but they sure were bad ugly. Knowing I would get some sort of response, I smiled and said, "Good evening, you lovely ladies." Miss America's response was, "Why don't you go fuck yourself."

I retorted, "Why don't you crawl under your rock, you ugly old hag." Her response, "Don't get vulgar with me," sent me into gales of laughter.

Now Bashful Betty opened up on me saying, "You're not exactly Prince Charming yourself, you know." It's now time for me to go into my act. I told her, "You hurt my feelings deeply knowing full well how delicate my feelings are. You're a nasty evil person."

That really built a fire under her and I was told that "I was a festering boil on the ass of the earth, and I was a dumb asshole." Then she really got serious, using every four-letter swear word she knew.

As I'm writing this, I recall my father's advice to me sixty years ago. He told me "Never make fun of anyone." The only way I can justify these nicknames to myself is to remember a rumor I heard that they all referred to me as "Crazy Larry."

Having accomplished my purpose, I had a drink or two, laughing to myself about the responses I got. I looked around and checked out the competition. There wasn't anyone I considered a serious threat for later that night so I want on my merry way.

It wasn't too long before I ran into my friend Swede. He was having a great time, drinking, romancing the ladies and all the things a logger does when he's out for fun. We brought each other up to speed on our progress from the night before and discovered we were both staying in the same hotel.

We hung around for a spell, had a few more drinks together and shared a few laughs. For some long forgotten reason, we decided the thing to do was to see if we could turn the bar upside down. The Swede was on one end and me on the other. We proceeded to attempt to pick up the bar.

All the patrons were leaning on the bar which made the job even more difficult. When the nails holding down the bar started to squeak, the bartender yelled, "Stop it, or you guys will have to pay for the damage, and neither of you will ever be able to darken this bar door again."

Knowing this wasn't an idle threat, we quit our endeavor and went on our separate ways.

I then proceeded to make the rounds of all the hot spots. By this time, I was beyond caring about running into my companion of the night before. Sure enough, it wasn't long before I saw her in one of the bars where she was draped around some fisherman like a cheap suit. I thought "Great, now I can rid myself of the guilt trip from the night before."

Onward to the Imperial Bar, the Pomoroy Club, Sweeney's, the Arctic Bar and the Top Hat. By now I've reached the indestructible stage. Occidental Bar, here I come. Who do I run into but a logger I will call Jimmy.

We knew each other from my Juneau escapades before I was on the Wrangell job. Had I not drowned my good sense with alcohol by then, I would have turned and left immediately. That boy was bad news.

There were all kinds of stories floating around about his actions. One of the tales involved his bidding on a timber sale out of Haines, Alaska. He got the bid. Now all he had to do was come up with the equipment to log it. No problem!

He went to the local equipment dealership on Sunday. Naturally, being Sunday, it was closed. He "borrowed" a truck with a lowboy trailer and loaded one of the dealership's D-8 cat on it. He was caught trying to load the truck and equipment on the Alaska

State ferry. His defense was, "I didn't steal it, just borrowed it. I certainly would have returned it after the job was complete."

The judge knowing he didn't always play with a full deck gave him a short jail sentence and let it go. How did the judge know about him?

It seems that Jimmy had been caught sending nasty letters to then Governor Egan. The Governor evidently knew Jimmy personally so he didn't push the issue. Governor Egan! Now, that's my idea of what a governor should be. He not only talked to the big businessmen all over the state, he would stop at the local bars and have a few drinks with the loggers and fishermen.

It's been said he had even gone down to the docks and had a few snorts of wine with the homeless natives who hung out there. I know Egan mingled and talked with the common people because my friend Swede still has his personal invitation to the Governor's Ball.

Has Alaska changed? It sure has. All of this happened during the 1960's. Now the current Governor is an ex-Okie oil worker. I'll just call him "Slick" because I'm guessing he used a quart of 40 weight motor oil every time he combed his hair. He wouldn't know a logging show from a girly show or a Silver Salmon from a herring.

His aim in life is to please the big oil companies. If he could convince the voters, I'm sure he would spend the permanent fund that is now rebated back to Alaskan residents. I'm sure if he had his way, he would build a bicycle path from Anchorage to Juneau. The fact that there isn't even a road there yet wouldn't faze that clown.

How in hell did I get off on that tangent? Time to get off the political stump and get back to the Occidental Bar.

My drinking partner, Jimmy, just loved to get me involved in fights he started. He would pick someone out of the crowd and start an argument with him. Just before he got hit, he would announce, "I can't whip you, but my partner can. He's got lots of horsepower." Jimmy would point me out.

I had saved his ass a couple of times before but not without some wear and tear on my clothes and body. This time, Jimmy's target was a big, burly, drunken native. I'm thinking to myself, "Oh, God, not again."

Unfortunately for Jimmy, this time he pushed too hard. Before he knew it, the native tied one on him, and I mean really nailed him. The native knocked him clear over the shuffleboard table and against the wall.

As Jimmy slowly slid down the wall, he yelled at me, "Take him, L.D. He can't hit very hard, he didn't even knock me down."

Now, it's my turn to either talk or fight. Possibly even both. The native was big and mad, so I thought I'd better try the talk method first. I knew I couldn't act scared, even if I was, nor could I act too eager. It's time for my "only if I have to" approach.

I explained to the big brawny native that I had nothing to do with the disagreement, didn't know whether I could whip him or not and didn't really care one way or the other. However, if I had to, I would give it all I had and at least move a little hide and maybe break a bone or two.

I was only 5' 11" weighing about 170 pounds, but was in excellent shape thanks to the Wrangell logging show. Two or three months on a high-lead show was better than a Charlie Atlas course. I don't think there would have been a very long line at the beach to kick sand in this boy's face.

My would-be opponent was still hot, but was still looking me over when his wife said, "He hasn't done anything to you. Sit your dumb drunken ass down." Luckily, he listened to his wife and sat down.

Now, it's Jimmy's turn. I went over, helped him up to his feet and explained very carefully the next time he pulled that stunt, the first thing I would do is kick his ass before doing whatever else I had to. Jimmy must have gotten the message because it never happened again.

I barhopped some more and ran into a fellow logger from Wrangell whose nickname was "The Pelican." You guessed it; he had a huge snot locker. He claimed part of the reason his nose looked like it did was my friend Swede had broken and rearranged his nose. He claimed the assault resulted over a song he had played over and over on the bar jukebox that had apparently pissed off the Swede.

The Swede didn't deny he was responsible for the nose job but swore there was more to the story than that. I always enjoyed seeing "the Pelican" as it made my oversize snooze easier to live with.

Knowing the next day was the Fourth of July and would be a great fun day; I decided to hang it up early and went to my hotel room. The great holiday arrived. Every fisherman and logger was in town with pockets full of money and their bodies overloaded with restless energy. Throw in a shipload of flatland tourists and almost anything can happen.

On the morning of July 4th, I was out and about early. Let the fun and games begin! It didn't take very long before I saw the first fight of the day. Almost every bar had a bell you could ring then yell "Timber." This meant you bought drinks for the house.

The disagreement occurred when it came time to pay for the drinks. A fisherman swore he rang the bell first, and he was going to pay. The logger was sure he was first, and no Goddamn fisherman was going to steal his turn. The fight was on.

Several windmill punches were thrown with little or no damage to either one. Finally the bartender came up with a Solomon-like solution. He suggested serving the house two rounds of drinks, and the fisherman and logger could put their money on the bar at the same time. They agreed.

I, of course, applauded the decision that resulted in two free drinks. The day had just begun. If one played their hand right, you could get toilet-hugging drunk and end up "talking to Ralph" by just going from bar to bar waiting for the bell to ring. Not me of course. By God, I had money to spend and sure as hell didn't have time to wait for any "stinking bell to ring."

I must have a mean streak running through me because one of the games I liked to play was to terrorize the tourists. Not all the tourists -- just certain types that you'll probably recognize.

I could spot them two blocks away. Either they wore shorts to show off their big hairy legs, a hooded sweatshirt, plus a jacket or they wore a ten-gallon hat on their half pint head, a loud cowboy shirt, with a belt buckle as big as a good-sized horse turd, that was almost concealed by their fat tummy. Of course, the picture isn't complete without the second type wearing a pair of "needle-nose, cockroach-stomper" boots.

It also helps if you wear a belt with your name on the back. You know, names like BuBu, Billy Ray, or George W. I had always wondered why these would-be cowboys did that until one day an educated logger explained it to me.

He told me the answer was really simple, "They wear belts with names on them in case they ever get their heads out of their asses, they will know who they are." His explanation made sense to me. It doesn't make you all bad if you dress like that; the deciding factor is the look on the tourist's face. The "get out of my way peon" look is what builds the fire in this boy.

I had two encounters with those types of tourists over the Fourth of July holiday. The first incident involved a guy in short pants and happened in the Red Dog Saloon. Oh, yes, there was one in Juneau complete with sawdust floors. It was a real tourist trap, which leads me to believe I may have been looking for trouble when I went in.

It was early in the day and I had a hangover that would kill an ordinary man. In walks Mr. Arrogant, stands beside me, and yells at the bartender. "I'll have a CC on the rocks." Being busy as hell, the barkeep paid no attention to his request. Again, only louder right in my ear, he yelled the same order, not requested, but ordered with the same result of being ignored. The third time did it for me.

With my head throbbing and my patience gone, it was time to act. I set my drink down, got up, grabbed him by the front of his jacket, and jerked him off the floor. I said, "I don't know where in hell you're from, but we don't do that in Alaska. You are being arrogant, obnoxious, and even loud, so shut up."

After a shake or two, I slammed him down. The lad wasn't as drunk as I thought or he decided he didn't really need another drink. Either way, as soon as his feet hit the floor, he beat feet.

The bartender laughed and said something like "Good job!" and bought me a drink. That action thinned the crowd out as the flatlanders left when they saw what could happen when you get out of line.

I saw there would be no need for more discipline so I took my act down the street a few doors. It didn't take very long and in walked Mr. Tough Cowboy. Again I was having a toddy and talking to a logger friend, proudly telling him how I had been forced to straighten out Mr. Hairy Legs.

There was just enough room at the bar next to me to for someone to squeeze in if he was careful. Unfortunately Mr. Tough Cowboy wasn't. He charged into the spot next to me, feeding me his shoulder to make more room for his fat belly.

The jostling caused my aching head to rumble and hurt again. It also made me spill part of my drink. Now that made me very unhappy. I jumped off the bar stool and said something unkind like, "Watch what you're doing, shit head."

He got that "How do you dare talk to me that way" look on his face. He went on to say "I've heard what animals loggers are. I can tell you're a logger, and you don't scare me at all."

Now, that was a mistake. I could see I would have to defend the honor of all the people employed in the forests. It was a nasty job, but someone had to do it.

My friend was taking in all this verbal exchange and kept saying things like, "Kick his ass and get it over with." I was in no hurry because I knew what the end result would be. Why not have a little more fun and let him talk his way in deeper and deeper.

He rambled on and on about how he used to be a boxer. My answer was short and to the point, "So, big deal."

His response was, "I still work out on the heavy bag." My answer to that comment was, "Since I haven't seen your old lady, I have no idea how heavy the bag is."

I knew it wouldn't take much longer as he was getting hot. I was right. He stepped back and yelled, "I'm going to punch you right in the nose." At the same time he was firing a big roundhouse punch at me. I could see it coming and had no problem moving my head out of the way and watched the punch sail by.

It's now my turn. I did what he said he was going to do, boom - right on the nose. Being pretty pleased with the results, I watched the blood flow as he landed on his fat ass. Thinking that was the end of the matter, my friend and I went back to our drinking and talking. We didn't even consider he might violate the Alaskan code of never calling the cops over a barroom brawl.

Wrong! He ran to the payphone and dialed the magic number 9-1-1. A few minutes later, two of Juneau's finest walked in, looking for a body, as that would be about the only reason to call them to a bar.

They were not pleased when this clown with a bleeding nose that was getting bigger by the second, rushed up and demanded they arrest poor little me for assault. The owner of the place rushed over, wanting to know what in hell was going on. "I saw the whole thing," he announced.

"This poor man (pointing at me) was minding his own business when he was attacked by him" while pointing at the one who blew the whistle. All the other customers agreed that I was just defending myself.

They were not pleased that an unwritten law had been broken and were wondering what kind of an asshole would do that. The other customers, the bartender and I were sure justice had been done when the offender was written up for disturbing the peace. The police hauled the villain off to jail. The nerve of that guy calling the police over such a minor thing as a broken nose.

I sure hope you don't get the impression that I was a bully. I never picked a fight with anyone smaller than me. I usually got along well with people I worked with unless pushed. I sure as hell didn't win every fight either. It's just more fun remembering the fights I won. If I could bat 500, I considered myself a winner. That's better than Ted Williams did.

The rest of that night is sort of a blur. I do remember I wound up at a party consisting of all natives, except me. That could have been where I got a reputation as a "teepee creeper."

The thing that sticks in my mind about the party was that just before the natives passed out, the drinkers would take a bottle with some booze left in it, sneak off and hide it. I sneaked around watching and remembering each hiding place.

One by one, they fell by the wayside until I was the only one left standing. I realized this meant the party was over. No use hanging around anyway as it was almost 7:00 a.m. and I had to catch a plane at noon that day.

Before I left, I couldn't resist the impulse to re-hide all their jugs. I sure would have liked to see the fun when they woke up and searched for their booze. I'll bet all hell broke loose.

I wandered down the street to a restaurant and forced some food down. After breakfast, I walked over to the hotel, picked up my gear and dragged it down the street to my office, the Imperial Bar. That was where we would be picked up for our trip to camp.

I must have had a better time than I remembered because as I was dragging my gear down the street, I met an elderly black man coming towards me. As he came up to me, he stopped, looked me up and down, and went into a laughing fit. He paused only long enough to say "Man, you sure is funny when youse is drunk."

What can I say? I must have given a real performance, maybe even a three-star rating. The Swede and I rated our time in town by our star rating system, 4 being the best. All there was left to do now was to have a drink or two and wait to be picked up for the trip to the camp in St. James Bay.

CHAPTER III

St. James Bay

Swede showed up at the Imperial Bar a few minutes before departure time. The bush pilot hauled our sick, sorry bodies to where we were loaded on a pontoon plane. We were on our way to another adventure in the great Alaskan outdoors at St. James Bay.

We arrived at St. James Bay after a short flight. The water was calm so we only bounced once or twice before gliding in to a short dock. We unloaded our gear and were met by the foreman, Ole.

He looked us over. It was clear that he was more than disappointed at what he saw. The fact that I damn near staggered off the dock while hauling my gear to dry land may have lead him to believe I liked to drink.

The first job they gave the Swede and me was to drill holes in boom sticks so they could be chained together when put in the water. The chained boom sticks prevent the logs from floating off.

The drilling equipment had a large chain saw motor on it. It had two handles, one on one end with the chainsaw motor on the other. It was like a machine a person would use to drill postholes, but instead of a ground auger, it had a three-inch wood drill bit. We drilled several holes without any mishaps until we ran out of gas for the motor while we were in the middle of drilling a hole.

The Swede filled the motor up with gas, locked the throttle wide open and gave the starting cord several jerks. It started with a mighty roar. The drill bit locked up in a knot in the boom stick, jerking the motor handle out of the Swede's hands and knocking him off the log.

Instead of the drill bit spinning into the boom stick, the motor and handle started to spin around wildly with the motor wide open. It looked like a small helicopter trying to take off. The handle and motor were going so fast there was no way we could reach in and unlock the throttle.

We watched it spin around wildly for a couple of minutes with a "What in the hell do we do now?" look on our faces. The Swede asked me "How long do you think it will take for the motor to run out of gas?" I responded "Too damn long" as I watched the foreman's pickup come into sight.

The Swede grabbed a peavey, a loggers hook with a spike at the end and crossed the stationary helicopter with it. This broke off the motor handle which in turn unlocked the throttle.

I can't remember what kind of song and dance we gave the foreman, but he didn't say much. He just gave us that look that said, "I knew I was right with my first impression when those two got off the plane."

It didn't take all that long to prove the foreman wrong as the Swede and I were both damn good workers as well as being excellent loggers.

As I said before, I'm not much on descriptive phrases but will give it a go. Breathtaking is the first word that comes to mind.

As you enter the deep blue cold water of the bay, you see the awesome sight of stands of huge Sitka Spruce trees separated by small tidal flats. The bay teems with King Crab, salmon, Dolly Varden trout, halibut, and on and on. There are fur-bearing seals, plain seals and sea otters.

In the back of the logging show was a receding glacier with snow-covered, sparkling blue ice. On the drive out to work, it wasn't unusual to see bears of all different colors. There were black bears, brown bears, cinnamon bears, grizzly bears and an occasional bear with a mixture of different colors. We also spotted wolves, eagles and moose.

St. James Bay was a real wonderland. Like I said, describing beauty isn't my strong suit, but hope you can understand why I fell in love with St. James Bay. All right, I know I'm here to "By God, log," and not just stand around looking at the scenery.

It's been said that to a logger there are only two good logging shows in the world, "The one you just left, and the one you are going to." However in this case I can truthfully say with a straight face that this really was a good logging show.

It had huge Sitka Spruce with no limbs until half way up the tree, very little taper, and besides they grew on flat ground. Some loggers have been known to say, there were lots of big trees, not many stumps, and the few stumps you saw were very small. Yes, that's a logger's fable, and I didn't believe it.

It wasn't long before we had a full crew and we were back to logging. The camp cook was heavy-set and a raspy old fart, but he was a very good cook. He was basically a meat and spuds kind of guy. There were four cat skinners, 4 chocker setters, a loader operator, a landing chaser, a log rafter, three timber fallers, one truck driver, a foreman, and the superintendent.

As the timber was all on flat ground, it was a real joy to work the show. The timber faller already had timber down, and we were ready to start logging. As usual, it took a day or two to work the kinks out.

It was a dry camp; in other words, no booze. One poor cat skinner had been in town too long and had a bad case of the DT's, or as called by folks in the woods, "delucious terribles."

The Swede had brought a pint of booze from town, in case of snake bite I guess. Seeing the poor cat skinner couldn't sleep and shook so bad, the Swede, humanitarian that he was, used his booze to help taper the poor fool off the sauce. In a day or two, the cat skinner was fine.

This is where I met George, a timber faller who was a relative of the camp push, Ole. This was George's first faller job. It seemed that if there were a stump near any tree he was falling, the tree would hit the stump destroying valuable timber.

My next job was being a choker setter. This means you attach steel cables, called chokers, onto logs and hook them to a cat to be dragged to a landing where they are loaded onto trucks. Choker setting wasn't a bad job, but it could be a bit dangerous.

One time after I had hooked my set of chokers to the cat, I was standing on a small log next to the skid trail that led to the landing. There was still a little snow on the ground and I didn't realize the log I was standing on crossed over another log and protruded onto the skid trail. The cat ran over the end of the log I was standing on, launching me about ten feet in the air. I still remember the look on the cat skinner's face as I was suddenly up in the air looking down at him.

The first thing a cat skinner and choker setter have to agree on is who is the boss of their operation. It has to be the choker setter because he can see where the logs are and has a better view of the whole layout than anyone else. Otherwise the poor choker setter will be deader than yesterdays' news.

I hadn't been at camp very long before I became known for my diplomacy and powers of persuasion. In less than a week, one of the other choker setters informed the boss man that he either worked with a different cat skinner or the boss could call him a plane as he was damn tired of running for his life. I had seen part of the action and knew what he was talking about.

Instead of watching for hand signals from his partner, the cat skinner would charge into the logs, knocking logs, limbs and anything in his way "Hell west and crooked" sending the choker setter running for safety.

For some reason the foreman knew I wasn't the timid type and asked me if I would give it a try and work with the wild cat skinner. He told me to "Do whatever it takes to straighten the dull shit out, or its town time for him."

My answer was the usual "Why not? I would try it for a day or two, but I needed to do it my own way." The foreman agreed.

The next morning we changed co-workers and trying to be fair, I explained to my new partner, Axel, the cat skinner, how it was going to be. I showed him the hand signals I used, and he was to watch me constantly. Axel nodded that he understood, and we were off.

The first turn of logs went fine. Then here he comes driving the cat full bore. I gave him the hand signal to turn around and back up towards me. Hell, no, the stupid ass charged forward.

Limbs and logs were flying, and I was running for my life. After yelling, throwing sticks and waving my arms, I got him to stop. That gave me just enough time to find a three-foot long spruce limb.

I climbed onto the cat, club in hand and explained to him, rather roared at him, that he was to do as I signaled or the next time I had to run, I would jump on the cat with another limb and beat his ears plumb off. That got his attention and the rest of the day went fine.

At day's end, my new co-worker told the boss what I had said and that he didn't want to work with me again. The foreman's answer was, "No way. You have two choices. It's either work with him or it's the highway."

We worked the rest of the season together and got along fine even though I had to throw a dirt clod at him occasionally to get his attention. The moral to this story is that a little diplomacy can go a long way.

It was pretty uneventful for a while, in fact until the Labor Day weekend. All the crew went to town except for the superintendent, the foreman and me. They had things to do at camp, and I needed a winter stake knowing I would blow a bunch of money if I went to town.

I explored the island on the first day, and did some fishing. I was amazed to find two almost rotten spruce stumps close to the bay. The trees had been chopped down many years before. I studied the scene where the stumps were located. They were close to the water, and the trees would have been the right size for a ship's mast.

I let my imagination run wild and could almost see a ship weathering a storm and making it to the protected waters of the bay. I tried to picture how they got the trees to the water, made the mast, and got it onto the ship. It sure gave me food for thought while I was fishing.

The next day I spent doing absolutely nothing except eating, sleeping, and resting knowing this would be the last break of the season.

The last day of the holiday was a beautiful sunny day. The superintendent and foreman were going to walk through the logging show to see what needed to be done and to see if they could locate a place to dig some gravel for the haul road. We were all good friends and being bored, I decided to tag along.

Everything was going fine until we had walked to the end of the haul road and angled off onto a trail through a dense alder thicket to look for a gravel deposit.

We were about a quarter of a mile down the trail when we heard a ferocious growl and smelled a horrible odor that I can only describe as somewhat like the odor of an old dog with bad teeth and breath.

Now the light comes on. We were on a trail through an alder thicket, most likely a bear trail, and now here comes the bear.

We stopped and looked at one another. Their eyes were big as turkey eggs, and I assume mine were too. What to do? Without a word, my friends and I spun around and started walking briskly back the way we had come.

Many thoughts were running through my mind. The foremost was, "If the bear charged out at us, could I outrun my companions?" All the while I was taking furtive looks over my shoulder looking for any sign of the bear. At the same time I was making sure my competition didn't get even half a step ahead of me. Yes, even a good friendship has its limits.

I knew full well that if one of us had started to run, it would have been the biggest stampede since the buffalo herds left the plains. We were about a mile and a half from camp, when I started to think about what my chances were if the bear charged.

The foreman and superintendent were both longer legged than I was, but I was a few years younger and in better shape. I had the additional advantage of wearing cork boots, and they were both slick shod.

Things were looking up for me. I was sure I could beat them out of the blocks and hold the lead for at least a hundred yards. Having read how fast a bear eats up ground while charging, I calculated the odds were in my favor.

Knowing all this didn't stop the hair on the back of my neck from standing on end, or stop me from sweating like a Georgia preacher on a hot summer's day. Looking at my companions, I could

**Loggers
flee
from bear**

see sweat pouring off their faces. As for me, the sweat was running down the crack of my ass like a river, but until I got home and checked my shorts, I couldn't even be sure it was all sweat.

They say animals can smell fear. If that's true, the bear must have been overwhelmed by the stench. After a quarter mile of fast walking and continually looking over our shoulders for the bear, we finally settled down and slowed our pace. Needless to say we reached the safety of camp in record time.

We talked the situation over after we got back to camp. The foreman and I decided we had to find out just how close the bear had been, and if possible to see how big it was. This time we wanted to be sure we could see from a safer vantage point. We fired up one of the cats and went to take a look.

Why didn't we take a gun with us? Who knows? The biggest gun in camp was a 30-06 that probably would have only made the bear angry even if we had shot and hit him. Besides, who needs a gun when you're as lucky as I am?

We drove the cat down the haul road, maneuvered through the thicket and made damn sure the bear wasn't anywhere in sight. We found the spot where the bear had been sleeping in a small sandy hollow. The hollow was about ten or fifteen feet from where we had started back down the trail on our hasty exit toward camp.

There was a huge bear track in the sand. I was wearing my round logger's hardhat, which was about 12" in diameter, and put it on top of the bear's track. The hardhat barely covered the track, leaving its claw marks uncovered. My guess is that he had been asleep, and we had wakened him. Whatever we did, it sure made Mr. Bear unhappy.

The rest of the logging season on my first trip to St. James Bay was pretty uneventful.

Winter Shutdown – Hazardous Trip South

The St. James Bay logging camp shut down for the season in mid-November. With a winter stake in my pocket, I grabbed the next plane out of camp into Juneau. There was just enough time to get a haircut and buy a few much-needed clothes before the state ferry headed south to Prince Rupert.

My body was weary so the easy trip on the ferry gave me a chance to recuperate and rest. It was snowing by the time I arrived at my friend's house where we spent the next two days visiting and telling stories.

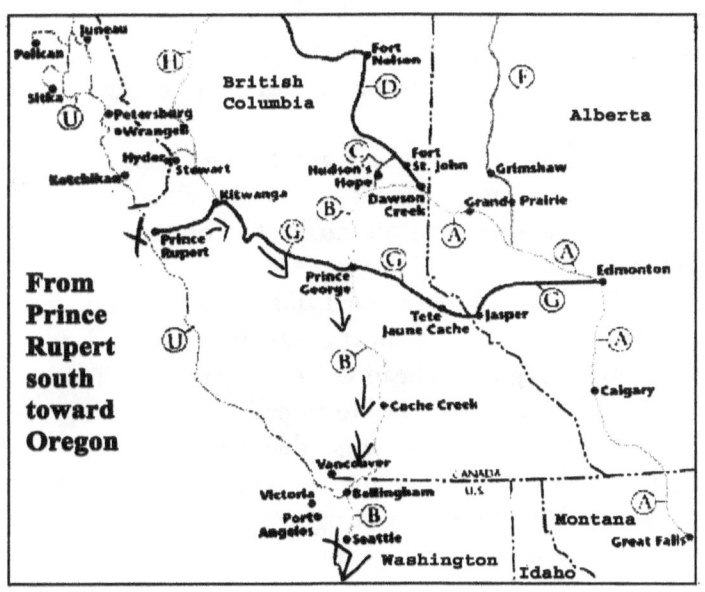

Finally it was time to jump in my car that I'd parked there last spring and start the approximately 1,425-mile drive south to Oregon. My logging partner, Swede, had decided to winter in Alaska, so this time the trip south would be solo.

The highway was a mess. It had snowed, melted, frozen and snowed again on top of that. Soon I reached the Frazier River Highway, but was way too busy concentrating on driving over the treacherous highway to even look at the scenery.

The first mishap, on what turned out to be a very eventful trip, happened while I was driving down a long, crooked and steep stretch of the highway. Somehow the front wheels of my car had settled into one pair of ruts and the back wheels in another. Now, I'm going downhill sideways 'hell bent for leather' putting on the brakes, turning the steering wheel back and forth, and even tromping on the gas pedal.

Nothing did any good, and the downhill sideway slide continued. Thank heavens, it was about 1:00 a.m. and there was no traffic at all on the highway.

I have no idea how far I slid that way, but it seemed like forever. A short tunnel finally came into view on the highway ahead while the car was still sliding sideways down the steep grade.

Whatever guardian angel that watches over fools and drunks came to my aid again. Evidently the front wheels had turned just right because the car straightened out just before the tunnel, and all was well.

Just as I reached the top of the hill on the Frazier River Canyon, my oil light came on. "No problem! There is extra oil in the trunk." I pulled over and checked the oil dipstick but it read 'full.' Re-checking the oil level showed the same results so figured the oil pump had quit.

It's still snowing heavily and the temperature is dropping. My guess is that it's about 20 degrees below zero. There's no traffic at all. Not having any idea how far it is to get help, I asked, "Why me Lord?"

Oh, well, there were plenty of clothes and a sleeping bag in the car so I bundled up, hopped back into the car and waited with the hope that someone would drive by. By now it's 3:00 am, and still not a vehicle in sight. There was nothing else to do except settle down and with any luck, get some shuteye.

I finally dozed off and woke up about 7:00 a.m. Still no sign of any traffic. By now, my patience had run out. I decided it was time to act, got out of the car and started looking for some help. After putting on a heavy jacket, the journey down the highway by foot began.

The temperature was as "cold as a whore's heart," and the walk soon turned into a jog. About three miles down the road, I saw what hopefully was the answer to my prayer. There was a small motel and restaurant ahead.

Soon a sign came into view that said "Closed for the Season" which made my heart drop. Then came a welcome sight. There was a 4-wheel drive pickup parked in front of the motel. Hopefully, that meant there was somebody there.

Hurrying to the front door, I began to knock loudly and was overjoyed when an elderly gentleman came to the door. After telling him my sad story, he invited me in for a cup of coffee. "Yes, there is a God," I said to myself.

After we discussed my problem, he volunteered to tow me to the nearest garage. It seems you meet the nicest people when you are most in need. An offer to pay him for the tow was refused. He wouldn't accept a red cent for his good deed.

After being towed to the garage, there was a short wait while the mechanic checked out my car. He determined the oil pump was working ok. There was lots of oil pressure so he figured the oil light must have shorted out. Anyway, my vehicle was now back in operation, and it was back to the highway again.

I drove steadily until about twenty miles out of Hope, British Columbia. It started to get dark so time to switch on the lights. Immediately, the motor started to miss.

Now it came to me what the red warning light had meant. Some idiot had switched wires on the warning lights for oil pressure and the alternator. It's still snowing and getting darker and darker in a hurry.

There was nothing to do but drive as hard as I could with no lights and hope for the best. My luck held and soon reached Hope. Yes, there is a town called Hope. Better yet, there was a garage and parts store still open. The mechanic there installed a new alternator, and it's back on the road again.

I was sure that the snow would change to rain close to the Canadian border. No such luck. It's still snowing, but I kept on driving as I was anxious to see my two boys again.

Just before reaching the border, a semi jackknifed across the road right in front of me. There was nowhere to go except into the snow berm.

My car rammed into the snow berm, passed the truck and went into a complete 360-degree skid before straightening out on the road. I pulled the seat cover out of the crack of my butt and headed for the border still determined to reach Florence, Oregon, before shutting down. I know I'm not very bright, but figured the snow had to change to rain soon.

There were no problems at the border this time, and I'm soon on I-5 headed south. It seems the farther I went, the louder the motor on my car roared so finally decided to pull into a rest area to check it out. It seems when the car rammed the snow berm, the neck of the exhaust manifold had cracked. By the time I stopped at the rest area, it had broken off completely. The big block V-8 was loudly talking to the world.

It was still snowing in Seattle. Suddenly, there were blue and red flashing lights behind me so I pulled over. "What now?" The state patrol officer proceeded with his lecture on the need for a better muffler.

I explained to him that the mufflers were fine, but the exhaust just wasn't getting to them because of the broken exhaust manifold. I related all the horrors of my trip to this point, and explained what had happened to the exhaust system.

The nice policeman asked how far I had to go, and how long it had been since I'd had any sleep. I told him about the short nap on top of the Frazier River pass.

He just shook his head and said, "Get your muffler fixed when you get to Florence. By the looks of you, you'll need plenty of noise to keep you awake." Yes, there are nice policemen. I know because I've met several.

I'm back on my noisy way again. The snow was still falling when I reached Portland. Somewhere between Portland and Salem, a Volkswagen Bug slid off I-5 and landed on its side in the medium. They were right in front of me when they overturned, so I immediately pulled over.

Leaving my motor running and roaring, I bailed out of my car just wearing a T-shirt and jeans, slammed the car door shut and went to see what I could do to help.

I climbed onto the side of the Volkswagen, opened the door and helped a young man, his wife and their baby out of the car. By this time, several cars had stopped. One kind soul offered to take the unfortunate travelers back to Portland.

After all the excitement, I suddenly realized it was bitter cold out in the wet snow and ran back to my car knowing it was toasty warm inside. My car was still running noisily, but unfortunately all the doors were locked with my keys still in the ignition. Another dilemma!

Luckily the trunk was unlocked because that was where the toolbox was stowed. I spied a large screwdriver that was just the right size to pry open the side vent window. Reaching through the vent window, I finally managed to unlock the door and quickly jumped in.

Turning the heater up another notch, I continued my journey over the snow-covered highway. The snow continued to fall all the way to Eugene, but that part of the trip was uneventful. I turned off onto Highway 126 with my goal for the day in sight and thought, "Thank God, only fifty more miles to Florence."

Twenty miles out of Eugene, Badger Mountain loomed into view. There was a truck and a car stalled halfway up the hill where they had spun out in the right-hand lane.

I stopped, backed up, looked the situation over and began to ponder the situation. "I have good snow tires on my car, I could see up the highway a good distance, the passing lane was clear, and I've come this far. Why not give it a go?"

Slowly building up speed, and seeing no other cars, I decided to "give it hell." The attempt was successful, so back to the road again. Finally, I saw the sign that said "Entering Florence." Yes, it was still snowing with lots of snow on the highway.

I made a short stop at Fisherman's Wharf, one of the local watering holes, for two or three toddies to calm my nerves. Only a few more blocks to drive and I'd be at my mother's house. After a short conversation with Mom, I crashed for about ten hours.

All the next day I spent visiting with Mom, telling her a few tales about my adventures. My mother was very broadminded so there wasn't any need to hold much back.

Later in the day, I drove to Reedsport, Oregon, to spend the night with my Dad. We went out on the town that evening and enjoyed a few drinks and laughs. The next day at 5:00 a.m., it was time to hit the road for the final lap of my journey to Talent, Oregon, as I'm really eager to see my sons again.

I arrived at 10:00 a.m. and had a great visit with the boys. They showed me their new bikes they had

71

bought with the money I'd sent them from Alaska. We went for a drive, stopped for hamburgers and then went to a wrecking yard where we located a used manifold for my noisy car. No, I hadn't fixed it yet, but the boys loved to hear it roar. Bedtime for the boys came way too soon, and it was time to take them home and leave.

Now, for a peek at my soft side. Just a short peek though, as I don't want to spoil my tough guy image. Driving away after dropping the boys off, my eyes began to mist over. My mask is slipping, and I know its time to get off the road soon. I made it to the next rest area and pulled way in the back where nobody could see me. I ripped off my tough guy mask and cried my heart out.

After cussing out the whole world, my ex-wife, myself, and maybe even saying a few bad words about God, I pounded the dash of the car, cried and cussed some more. This all took about an hour.

Finally settling down, the tough guy mask was put back on, and strapped on tight. Now my weepy blue eyes turned to a blazing steel blue, and I said out loud, "Fuck the whole world. Someone is going to pay for this."

It was time to head back to Reedsport and the nearest bar, probably The Rainbow that was a hangout for rough and tough loggers and mill workers. I remember hoping that someone would say something to start a fight, like maybe "Hello."

Hopefully this unmasking episode will help explain to family and friends why there weren't as many trips made to see the boys as there should have been, but even tough guys can bear only so much emotional pain.

CHAPTER IV

Return to St. James Bay

It's now May and I'm restless as hell. Time to return to the place where a person can do almost anything he feels big and strong enough to do, so long as he does it honestly. Alaska, here I come again!

The car is ready for the long trip back. The Swede had called and told my Dad that the St. James Bay logging show was ready to roll so I made one last trip to see the boys. It was a repeat of the first visit; only worse knowing it would be months before seeing them again. My gear is loaded in the car and it's time to take off for the solo trip north.

The drive of 1,425 miles to Prince Rupert was etched in my mind and planned to make only one overnight stop before getting to Prince Rupert to catch the ferry. This may be hard to believe knowing my luck on the trip down, but everything went according to 'Plan A.'

There were no problems on the trip up even though the roads were pretty broken up and muddy in spots because of the spring thaw. However, that was nothing compared to the icy, snow covered roads on the trip down.

As soon as I arrived in Prince Rupert on the following day, I picked up an Alaskan ferry schedule. There was enough time for a one-day visit with my friend before catching the next ferry to Juneau. As usual for that time of year, the ferry was almost empty so there was lots of room to put my gear and crash. As I was almost broke, I spent most of the trip enjoying the scenery.

Occasionally a bear was sighted on the shore searching for almost anything to eat, mainly grass and skunk cabbage this early in the season. There was a deer or two, skinny as hell from a long winter, and, from time to time, a killer whale would act as an escort to the ferry.

Hell, it's not all that bad being hard up for cash. I had enough money for a hot dog when I got hungry and coffee to warm me up while nature gave me a continuous free show.

After the ferry made stops at Wrangle, Ketchikan, and Petersburg, there it was dead ahead, Juneau. "What, no bands? Maybe they didn't know I was coming." Oh well, life goes on.

The first stop in Juneau of course is my office, the Imperial Bar. The owner gave me a big welcome by saying "Oh Christ, not you again?" He went on to tell me that "Yes, St. James Bay is hiring. The Superintendent is in town and the Swede is already out there at camp."

It's time to make my move. I'm informed the logging camp now had an office in town and was told where it was located. I toss my gear in the back room of the Imperial Bar, and hotfoot it to the logging camp office. Dan, the superintendent, was there. After a brief greeting, he hired me on the spot. He went on to tell me there was a plane hauling supplies headed for camp in two hours, that I should catch it and go to work. See, my luck isn't always bad.

Time is short and so is my cash supply; barely enough for cigarettes and a few other necessities. No razor blades included because it's time to grow a beard again. The supply plane landed in St. James Bay and floated up to the dock. Who should appear but my friend, the Swede.

After unloading the supplies and my gear from the plane, we hauled it all into camp. The Swede and I played catch-up on what went on in our lives during the winter shutdown. First of all, the Swede asked about his mother who lived in Reedsport and was dating my Dad.

After reassuring him that his mother was fine, my Dad was doing great, and they were both happy and healthy, the subject switched to what his life had been like over the winter. He told me the ups and downs of his love life, sometimes the lack thereof, and what the town barflies, male and female, were up to.

Now, it's my turn to tell the Swede about my conquests and failures. Of course, he knew everyone in Reedsport and the surrounding area. When telling him of one or two of my conquests, he always made me feel good by giving me the big smile and saying, "Been there, did that." That always ruined my day as I was sure that most barflies were virgins until they met me.

The story the Swede got the biggest kick out of was about the time I got aced out by another woman. You may as well share his laughter at me too. Why should you be any different?

The story started when Dad and I were having a few drinks on a Saturday night at The Rainbow Bar in Reedsport. In walks a good-looking blond followed by a husky, mean-looking, dark-haired woman wearing a black leather jacket. They sat down at a table nearby and ordered drinks for themselves. Now is the time to turn the charm on full bore, and I told Dad to watch this action.

I strolled over to the table and asked the blond to dance. The band was playing a lot of slow shit-kicking music. Well, maybe not good music, but slow and loud. My idea of dancing is sort of walking around on the dance floor while holding my partner close while we danced. When the dance was over, the blond honey came back to the bar with me. Of course I bought her a drink and winked at Dad as if to say, "See, that's how it's done."

About that time, the big, husky brunette rushed up to the bar, grabbed me by the shoulder and said in a loud, nasty voice, "That's my woman. If you don't leave her alone, I'll take you outside and kick your ass." What to do now?

If I even considered trying to kick her ass, every logger in the bar would want a piece of me for hitting a woman. If she would whip me, I would be laughed out of town. This was a no-win situation. It was time to withdraw and regroup. Dad thought the whole episode was funny as hell. So, guess I'm not much of a lover, but being able to entertain folks isn't all that bad.

Soon the crew is assembled and it's time to log. The first week or two, it was back to setting chokers. For some reason, the boss decided I should chase the landing and second load. This meant I would unhook the chokers and cut off limbs that still remained on the logs. Then it was time to climb on the cab of the truck and give signals to the loader operator on where to set the logs on the truck. This was a great job, busy all the time. As the old saying goes, "Busy hands are happy hands."

For some reason the boss decided he needed someone to fill in wherever help was needed. That sounded like my cup of tea. Filling in as a truck driver, second loader chaser, log rafting or choker setting would mean more hours and more money. What more could anyone want?

My next job at the camp was rafting the logs. A good job, but you had to work during high tides, day or night. The logs were bundled and dumped on the tide flats during low tides. My job was to string boom sticks around the bundles to keep them from floating away. Boom sticks were long logs chained together to make a log corral. You didn't want to fall in the water, as it was freezing cold.

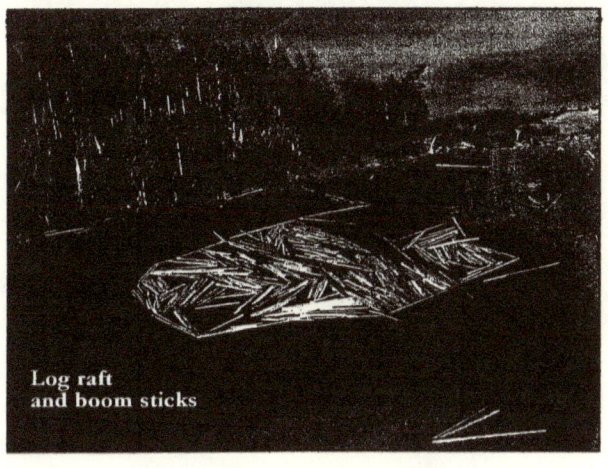

Log raft
and boom sticks

Someone had flown Jet, a Black Labrador, to camp. Jet soon decided he belonged to me and became my constant companion. He would follow me around on the boom sticks.

I, of course, had cork boots and would try to dump him in the water by spinning a boom stick one way and quickly reversing the spin. That dog could have his front feet going one way and his back feet going another. I never could dump him.

Talk about an exciting dog's life; Jet certainly had one. There was a family of sea otters under our log deck, and he loved to chase them.

The odds of his catching one were 12 to one, so you can guess who won. Poor Jet would run after the otters until he dropped from exhaustion, gasping for air with his tongue hanging out like a red necktie. The otters would all run out, gather around Jet and chirp at him. After a while the poor dog couldn't stand it. Somehow Jet would gather enough energy to go again, and the race was on.

One day Jet made the mistake of jumping into the bay to try to catch one. The otters were on his head, his back and all over him like ugly on ape. I'm sure he would have drowned if I hadn't thrown rocks and dirt clods to distract the otters.

Poor Jet had one more life-threatening experience on the mud flats. I was getting ready to raft the logs when I saw a good-sized wolf trotting across the flats. So did Jet. I could almost hear him thinking, "Oh boy, something new to chase."

He blasted off toward the wolf. Jet got about half way there when the wolf turned and started to run towards him. Jet made a smoking U-turn and headed back to me, running twice as fast as he did on his outbound trip. The wolf chased him to within fifty feet from me, turned around and just trotted off. Needless to say, Jet decided to stay close to me the rest of the day.

One day while I was rafting logs, the tide went out about 1:00 p.m. I decided to get a cup of coffee at the cook shack and maybe grab a nap. I walked from the log dump to the cook shack. I saw the cook leaning against the sill by an open window. He was humming a tune with no idea anyone else was around. He was wearing a pair of heavy-duty logger suspenders.

I reached through the open window, grabbed the suspenders, and let go. Wham! He jumped straight up in the air and came down landing on his feet. Then he went down to his knees, gasping and coughing.

All sorts of horrible thoughts were going through my mind. The first being, "My God, I killed the old fool." I knew it would be at least three hours before I could get a plane in to get him to the hospital. What to do?

Thank God, he solved the problem for me. He got to his feet looking confused. I decided to forget about coffee or a nap and get out of there fast. I ran into the nearby woods and hid, watching to see what would happen next.

It wasn't long before he came out of the cook shack and looked around. He walked over to search the bunkhouse and all the other out buildings, still looking puzzled as hell.

I walked back to the log deck and waited for a log truck to come in. I finally caught a ride out to the logging show and worked the rest of the day telling no one about the near disaster. When work was over and dinnertime came around, I filed in with the rest of the crew with my best innocent look on my face.

The cook eyed us all suspiciously, but not a word was said. I still don't know what he thought happened, whether it was possibly a daydream, an alien attack, or just his imagination. I escaped again! Did it make me stop my stupid pranks? Only for a short time.

I think this is as good a time as any to explain what a small fly-in logging camp is like. The camp at St. James Bay was deluxe compared to others I have worked in. The camp had electricity furnished by a big diesel driven generator. We had hot water showers, and even a washer and dryer. The bunkhouse had electric lights but weren't used much as we had 18-hours or more of daylight in the summer.

St. James Bay Camp

The timber fallers had a bench set up for filing the chains for their saws. The bunkhouse had a single bed for each logger, with a spare bunk or two, and make shift lockers for each. Sheets were changed and washed by the cook's helper. All in all, not a bad life.

St. James Bay Camp

There was a separate room for the superintendent and foreman, and the cook and his helper had their own room in the cookhouse.

The cook had much to do with whether a camp was considered good or bad. Of course, if he was considered undesirable, he or she was soon on the next plane headed for town. Our first cook at the camp claimed to be a French chef and lasted only about ten days. He served too much green stuff like salads and fluffy pastries.

By God, we wanted meat and spuds, apple pie, cookies for the spike table with leftover roasts and ham, and freshly baked bread. In other words, food that built up your horsepower and would stick with you for a strenuous 12-hour shift. Breakfast was always a hearty meal with eggs, hot cakes, bacon, toast, juice, coffee and plenty of it.

What did we do for entertainment? Very little. I played cribbage with the Swede or anyone else that could stand my constant harassment. We traded lies about our adventures. No, I wasn't always able to tell the biggest fables, but was always in the top finalists.

A camp rule banned poker and any type of gambling as it could lead to fights and hurt feelings. The fact that we were usually tired as hell by day's end and needed the sack time, kept camp life as boring as this chapter trying to describe it.

We kept in contact with the outside world with a CB radio. This meant if your wife or sweetheart called you, everyone in southeast Alaska heard you. Not all the callers knew that, so you best be on good terms with your honey when you left town or everybody on the air heard what a no good, chippy-chasing, drunken bad boy you really were. There were the other callers who were too sweet. Either way, you were the brunt of bad jokes for some time.

I once received a call from a lady in town telling me I was a celebrity. It seems I had words in a bar with a clown, Vern something or other, who had a morning radio show. In order to express myself and make a point, I had jerked him off a barstool. The next morning on his radio show, he informed the world that a certain logger from St. James Bay had better be careful the next time he came to town.

How he knew I had left town that soon, I don't know. The lady that called said I'll bet that was you, wasn't it? Another mystery, how did she guess? I recall another call about how sweet I was, but won't go into that. That's life in a logging camp.

Oh how time does fly. It's the Fourth of July already. No matter how much I hate to, I'll be forced to go to town. Why? Because it's what all good loggers do. The truth is, I was second in line for the plane, behind the Swede of course.

Tension builds up in camp and shows its ugly face in town. It seems one of the choker setters had a bone to pick with me. Believe it or not, I was completely unaware of his feelings. It seems the constant teasing and laughing got his goat. No sense of humor I guess. The gist of the story was I guess the choker setter and his cat skinner, a big brawny native named Leonard, had made plans to teach me a lesson when we got to town.

I was in the bar when the choker setter hopped in my face, telling me what a beating I was about to get. Not having had time for more than one drink, I tried to laugh it off. No way. The big native threw in his version of what was going to happen. It's obvious I'm in deep shit. Then the answer to my dilemma walked in the door, the Swede.

One glance tells my hero the story so he strolled over and asked what the problem was. I explained what had happened. The Swede's answer was simple when he told Leonard, the cat skinner, "You and I are just going to watch, or you will be too damn busy with me to see anything anyway."

Leonard just nodded yes that he understood. Now it's one on one. The poor choker setter knows deep down that even on a good day, he couldn't whip half of me. The day was looking pretty gloomy to him now. After spouting a few words like "I'll catch you later," he bolted out the door.

Hell, it's too early in the holiday to fight, and anyway now things had turned out fine. Laughing, I thanked the Swede, bought him a drink, and we were off on our separate paths to bigger and better things.

I'm about to tell you about the worst drinking binge of my life. It's not an incident in my life that I'm proud of, and still can't understand why I did it. However, I feel if I can tell stories on other people, it's only fair to include myself.

As I sit here remembering about the good old days when men were men and women were glad of it, I think to myself, "You damn old fool, how come you're still alive." Just lucky I guess. To prove the point, I'll tell you about one of my trips to Juneau.

It was over the Labor Day holiday. I had money in my pocket and was full of piss and vinegar. It's a memory I'd just as soon forget, but it was a lesson in my life. I feel that if I'm going to tell the good, the bad should be included.

It started out as the usual Juneau holiday drunk. Of course, it all started at the Imperial Bar. The Swede and I cashed our checks and told each other how great we were. We parted company and the Swede went one way and I the other.

I checked out the Occidental Bar. No action there, so time to head for the Pomeroy Club. Oh yes, lots of action at the Pomeroy as there were a bunch of loggers there from all over. Some of them with a head start on me with the booze.

I'd known this logger Bill for a while and knew he was almost as crazy as me. He and this native chick were drunker than hell when he spotted me coming in the door. Bill yells out, "Hi, L.D., watch this." Couples have been known to do "it" in the rest rooms. He yelled out, "I'm going to take this old girl right here on the shuffleboard."

As he is talking, he is pulling up her skirt and pushing her backwards onto the shuffleboard table. All the time, the chick has this big grin on her face. Not being much on watching, I said maybe you had better rent a room. Now Bill has everyone's attention. He proclaims that, "No, by God, I'm going to make history here."

About that time, the bartender, spoilsport that he was, put an end to a performance that would have well been worth four stars.

I continued to drink all that day, all that night, and continued on into the next day. I don't know why; I just did. About 2:00 p.m. the next day, I'm in bad shape. The Swede and his honey, Nancy, and a friend of hers, don't remember her name, came into the bar I was in. They decided to put me in the back booth to sleep.

By now I have a bad case of the shakes. In fact, I'm spilling more than I'm drinking. I guess I had the DT's. Anyway, I knew it was time for me to quit drinking and get some rest. The only problem was that every time they tried to get me to lie down, I wanted to take my clothes off. I would take them off, and they would put them back on.

After a time they gave up on that plan, and soon decided they'd best check me into the Franklin Hotel. Not the best hotel in town. but I had stayed there before. They got me on my feet, out the door, and out to the street steering me to the hotel. Now comes the problem.

The last time they put my pants on, they had zipped them up, but didn't fasten the top button. Down come my pants, and down I go. Then the heavy set native friend of the Swede's honey, trips over me and down she goes right on top of me. What a sight!

Of course, the streets are loaded with flatland tourists. Thank God, I had on clean underwear. I bet the flatlanders still talk about the sight. Yes, that's a story that isn't told very often. However, when this book was in the planning stage, it was my intent to include the good, the bad and the boring.

After getting back on my feet and pulling my pants up, off to the hotel we went. I remember lying there in bed vibrating for three hours before I finally went to sleep for about 12 hours. Yes, I learned the lesson of when to stop drinking and I never did that again. No, I'm not proud of that binge, but it happened.

After that blow out, I still had two more days of the holiday left. I decided to rent the room for the rest of my stay even knowing I would never over train like that again. I just spent the rest of my time in town making the rounds, drinking, romancing all the honeys in town, not even looking for trouble, and turning in by midnight every night.

The room I rented in the Franklin Hotel had two beds. The hotel itself was built into the hillside. My room was on the second floor and was just about window high beside the bank. A logger friend, I'll call Fred, had asked if he could share the room with me if he didn't have a place to stay. My answer was "Hell, yes," as I might need a favor from him sometime.

About 2:00 a.m., my window opened and here is Fred with the ugliest native woman I had ever seen. Knowing what was going to happen next, I went to the hotel lobby and drank coffee for an hour or so. I went back up to my room knowing full well it doesn't take a logger very long to get a job done. Yes, the job was complete. Fred asked me if I wanted to give it a go. I said, "Thanks, but no thanks."

He proceeds to get his love of the night dressed, opened the window, grabbed her shoulders and the ass of her pants, fired her out the window, and slammed it shut. To add insult to injury, he pulled down the shades. What a way to end a romance.

Afterwards, I laughed myself to sleep after Fred and I turned in for the night. The next morning Fred and I got up and went to get some breakfast. Fred had to listen to my chuckling about how ugly his darling was. I said, "Hell, Fred, she didn't even have any teeth."

His answer was "Yes she did, two on one side." That cracked me up again. Then guess who comes down the street, but the love of his life.

I spotted her first and told him "Here comes your honey, Fred. He said, "No way, she wasn't that ugly." I told him, "Oh yes, that's your sweetie all right, isn't she a dandy?"

As she gets closer to us, she flashes a toothless smile and said sweetly, "Hello, Freddie." That did it. I had to hang on to a parking meter because I was laughing so hard.

As soon as I caught my breath, I looked at him, smiled, said, "Hello, Freddie," and burst into gales of laughter again.

About that time Fred had all that fun he could stand and decided to pass on breakfast. He felt he needed a drink more than my company. I saw that poor man several times after that, and always greeted him with a big smile and a "hello, Freddie."

His usual answer was, "Shut up, you S.O.B." So I survived another trip to Juneau, and now it's time for an uneventful trip back to the logging camp routine.

I was still rafting logs and doing whatever else was needed around the camp. By now the crew was used to each other, and most problems had been taken care of.

The only unusual event I remember during that stretch at St. James Bay was that some logging magazine had sent a camera crew out to camp to take pictures of our cat logging operation. I was second loading at the time and the landing was a sea of mud.

The loader operator and I were not what you would call great friends. It seems we always had different opinions on which log should go where on the trucks. Seeing that I had the final say, he didn't like it much. So I guess it was time for revenge.

As the cameras were rolling, he grabbed a log, and swung it, not too gently, knocking me off the cab of the truck into the mud hole. The camera crew, the loader operator and the truck drivers all thought it was funny as hell. Not me.

I never saw the film they shot and don't know whether it had even been developed. If there had been an audio part, I'm sure it would have been bleeped out in its entirety.

Luckily I landed on my head, or I could have been badly injured. I was forced to give the loader operator a list of things, none of them good, that would happen to him if it should ever occur again.

Winter Break – South to Oregon

Logging season is over. It's time for my annual trip south for the winter. I stopped at my friend's place in Canada, picked up my car, drove down to Oregon, saw my boys, went through my cussing and crying period, and finally settled down in Reedsport with my Dad.

I'd had a good season in Alaska and was drawing unemployment. I'll use the excuse that logging jobs in the winter are hard to find and that the temptations of taverns and bars are everywhere. Besides that, there were all those lovely ladies to chase down south. I couldn't let them down, could I? By God, that was part of my job.

To make sure my funds would last until spring, I chased and snagged a honey who was a bartender. Now a big chunk of my expenses were taken care of. I drank at the bar where she worked, and, of course, received lots of free drinks. The plan was to lay a five-dollar bill on the bar, but she would only take it when the owner was there.

Not being stupid, the owner knew what was going on. He finally told her, "For Christ's sake, don't take his money just because I'm here, I should be paying him a salary. He's always here late at night so I don't have to worry about anything bad happening to you girls; besides he helps restock after closing. God, you girls must think I'm dumb."

I did have a new experience this trip. It was the first time I was given just 24 hours to leave town. I occasionally strayed while my lady friend was working and had taken out a local clown's lady friend a couple of times. Apparently this made him a little upset.

After drinking several shots of fighting whiskey, and with a couple of friends in tow to either back him up or pick him up, the clown gave me the word, "Leave town in 24 hours or you will be in real trouble."

I thought it was funny as hell, but didn't want to laugh and hurt his feelings. It's time to negotiate. I told him I understood how he felt and promised I wouldn't go out with his honey again, but I explained the woods in Alaska didn't open up for awhile and asked him for a 30-day extension.

He thought it over and decided, "O.K., but no more than 30 days." He was happy, I thought it was funny, and life went on.

My Dad was working at the International Paper mill in Gardiner at the time. I didn't see very much of him as our hours were different. On weekends, we would bar hop. One of the advantages of him being with me was the fact he also received free drinks at my lady friend's bar.

CHAPTER V

Another Season Begins at St. James Bay

The winter break is over and it's time for one more trip to see the boys before I go back up to St. James Bay to log.

I've often been asked "Don't you get lonely in camp?" Of course we did. But where there's a will, there's a way to get rid of frustration. A long-time tramp logger once told me his cure for loneliness during long months in camp. He claimed there were two ways that always worked for him. One was painful as hell, and the other had some serious side effects.

The painful way was to open the bunkhouse window, lay "it" on the sill and then slam the window down. Painful, but effective. The other way was to take care of the problem by hand in the shower.

The side effect of the shower solution was that for weeks afterward, every time it rained, he would have an erection. This may well explain why the lonely women in town held a rain dance just before the loggers arrived. Yes, I admit I've always been a bit crude.

I settled into the daily routine of working long days for several months at the St. James Bay camp. Before I knew it, Labor Day rolled around and it was back to town for some R. & R. After my last trip, I was going to change my ways and did.

One of the new guys in camp was married and had a house in town. His wife worked as a secretary in town for the Department of Education. She had a girl friend who had just recently divorced and who wanted to meet a "real logger." Blind date time. After thinking about it, I said, "Hell, why not?" What did I have to lose even is she was a real bowwow.

I arrived in town, cashed my check and didn't even have a drink. After getting a haircut, I bought some new slacks and a nice sweater determined to play my role as a gentleman. I was to meet my friend, his wife and the surprise package in a nice club at 7:00 p.m. It's now 5:00 p.m., two more hours to wait.

"What the hell, a drink or two couldn't hurt anything." Yea, right! I went to my usual hangout and who do I see but an old girl friend. She's happy as a pig in mud. "Oh Larry, I heard you were in town and I've been waiting for you." Not wanting to burn any bridges, it's dilemma time.

Looking her over, I could see she had been drinking while she waited. She had three stages while on a date beginning with dull and boring. After "x" number of drinks, she became fun and exciting. She's now at that point, but I know a few more drinks and she would be at the mean and impossible stage. Kind of like a timber rattlesnake in August when they are shedding their skin, mean and quick to strike.

I looked at my watch. Yes, I have time so bought her several drinks while I nursed mine. I could tell the third stage was there so said something I knew she wouldn't like and the fight was on. It ended by her saying, "If you don't like the way I am, get out of here and find someone else." My plan had worked. I stormed out of the bar and yelled back at her, "By God, I will."

I hailed a cab, arriving at the club at 7:00 p.m. sharp and strolled in. I looked around and there they were. My blind date is a knock out and said my "Please God don't let me screw this up" prayer. I take a deep breath, turn my charm up to the highest level, walk to the table, hoping she doesn't make a break for it, introduce myself, and the show is on.

After a few drinks and dinner, my friend and his wife excuse themselves, saying they had to get home and take the babysitter home. Things are rolling along fine in spite of the fact that one of my logger friends going by, stopped and said, "Jesus Christ, is that you L.D.? It's the first time I've seen you with a white woman."

I laugh it off and I say those damn friends of mine will say anything to embarrass me. The lady and I have a few more toddies and made idle chitchat, while I contemplated my next move.

The spell is broken by the arrival of my logging superintendent accompanied by some clown I didn't know who was wearing a suit. We invited them to sit down. Bad move. Dan, my superintendent, sat down by me, and Mr. Wonderful sat next to my date.

At first glance, I was sure I wouldn't like him. Maybe it was the suit. It was sort of a horse blanket plaid that no respectable horse would be caught dead wearing. We ordered drinks and I out fumbled them.

Dan introduced his partner as the purchasing agent for the company. The suit pulled out his wallet to pay for the drinks making sure he displayed a folder of credit cards as long as a well rope. We chat and laugh for a while and the credit card man's hands are no longer on the table.

My date leans over and whispers in my ear, "Larry, this guy is bothering me. He won't keep his hands to himself." You have to remember that I am playing the part of a gentleman, not a logger, so I whisper back, "Don't worry babe, I'm about to take care of this."

Dan knows something is going on and things are about to happen, which it does. I turn to the purchasing agent and said, "With all those credit cards, do you have something like Blue Cross that will take care of broken bones and a long stay in the hospital?" No answer. "Because if you don't, you best keep your damn hands on the table."

A long silence. The suit turned to Dan and said, "Doesn't this guy know who I am? He can't talk to me like that."

Dan turned to him and said, "Yes, he knows who you are and doesn't care. Yes, he can talk to you like that because I've seen him in action."

The clown walked out with a "I can't believe this happened to me!" look on his face. Dan laughed and shook his head and remarked he had better go find the fool before he got himself killed.

Not wanting to go into any more details, I will just say I spent the rest of the holiday with the knockout. I guess it was my reward for being a gentleman.

Time to go back to camp knowing this coming session of logging will finish the job at St. James Bay. We have logged most of the good ground. Now we have some good timber left, but it's on muskeg which is another word for a swamp. Most people think muskeg and the tundra are one and the same. Not true.

Tundra is frozen ground called permafrost with a layer of vegetation like moss, small bushes, flowers, etc. growing over it. When the layer of vegetation is broken, the permafrost is exposed to the summer heat that leaves big trenches that get deeper year after year. That's the reason work on the tundra is either done in winter, or on gravel roads with insulation under the gravel.

Muskeg on the other hand is soft ground with a layer of vegetation over it, sort of like a mat made up of roots, plants, etc. If you break through the mat, you sink like a rock. There are places on the Alcan Highway where D-8 caterpillars sank out of sight, and they just built the road over the top of them.

We log what is left on the good ground while waiting for the ground to freeze. Now it's muskeg time. If you don't make any sharp turns or spin the tracks on the cat, everything is fine. With the crew cut down, I'm back to setting chokers.

We all know that what you don't want to happen always does. One of the cats starts to go down. After being careful not to spin the tracks, you look around for a big tree or stump if there is one close enough. You pull the winch line out to the anchor spot, hook up, take out the slack and see if you can pull the cat out which is slowly going down.

If that doesn't work and it usually doesn't, you run and get another cat and send his choker setter to round up the other cat. At least the winch line will hold the cat up long enough to have something to hook to. When the other cats arrive, they run their winch lines out and hook to whatever is above the mud line. Now at the right time, they slowly pull using only their winches.

Suddenly, you hear a sucking sound and then a plopping noise that sounds sort of like when you jerk a pacifier out of a baby's mouth. The mud has lost its grip, and you're home free.

This happened over and over again until the snow got deeper and deeper. By the first of December, we were done. It's goodbye forever to beautiful St. James Bay.

I spent a few days with the knock out, but Christmas is coming, and the desire to see my boys can no longer be pushed back. I leave Juneau to head south. The knock out goes the same way as St. James Bay, never to be seen again.

CHAPTER VI

Haines

Winter is over and now it's Alaska time again. The logging is finished at St. James Bay, and it's time to display my talents elsewhere. My starting point is again Juneau.

I spent a day or two checking around. My job information source, the Imperial Bar, tells me that Haines is the place to go as they are short of loggers there. Haines is a short run on the Alaskan Ferry system.

I arrive on a Friday afternoon and check at a bar or two. Yes, I find out there is a cat logging show at a fly-in camp on the Sullivan River, and they need a choker setter desperately. Knowing the best way to get in touch with the boss is through the flying service they use. I found out that it was Bennett's Air Service whose owner was an old bush pilot and a damn good one.

He gets on the radio and talks to the owner about my job search. Yes, the owner has heard about me and hired me in spite of it. I guess he really was desperate.

The job was a great cat logging show, but the camp was crude and pretty primitive. When you couldn't stand your own body odor any longer, you took your soap and towel, went down to the bay, jumped in, jumped out, soaped up, jumped back in to rinse off and jumped back out as quickly as possible to dry off. God, that water was cold.

Somehow in the first two weeks there, I hurt my back. Oh God, the pain. It hurt so damn bad I couldn't even put my work boots on. The owner's 13-year-old son helped me put them on in the morning and would take them off at night.

Thank God while he was looking through things other loggers had left at the camp, the boy came up with a back brace some other unfortunate logger had left. I started wearing it and slowly the pain went away. I can still remember the pain though.

While dragging chokers through the brush, each time the choker hung on something, which seemed like every other step, I would damn near, and sometimes did, yell with pain.

Why didn't I go to town to see a doctor? I was afraid the season would be over before I could work again, and I needed the money. Besides that, I was a tramp logger and, by God, we were tough. Stupid too, I guess.

We finished that job and went to town where the owner had started a high-lead logging show. Although working out of town wasn't my thing, I wanted to finish the season and have a road stake.

The owner hired a tong setter. It was a hog-wire outfit from Montana but they lacked modern equipment. They had a huge cold deck of logs and loaded the trucks out of the deck while logging at the same time.

My job was to catch the tongs the loader operator threw in mid air. The loader operator would spin the machine around, taking his foot off the brake, utilizing centrifugal force, the tongs would fly through the air. When the tongs got almost to me, he would gently apply the cable brake.

The tongs weighed ten or fifteen pounds. The only way I can describe the tongs is they looked like an oversized set of old-fashioned ice tongs. I would grab the tongs, pick out a log, set the tongs, and run like hell.

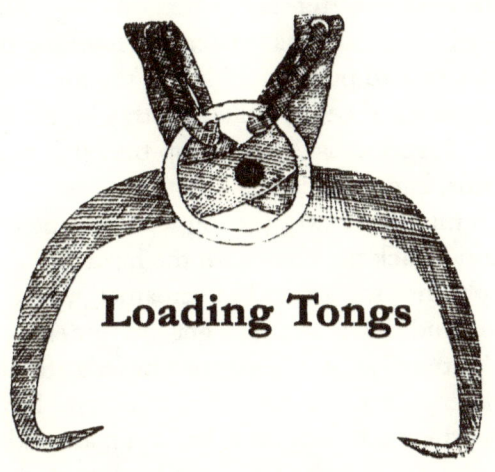

Loading Tongs

Yes, the job was dangerous. You had to have excellent reflexes and very little in the smarts department. Yes, I was their man. Before I go any further, I best tell you what happened to the man I replaced.

He was on top of the log deck when the mainline of the high-lead show snapped. The line whipped back, wrapped itself around the poor guy, uncoiled and threw him about thirty feet. When the line uncoiled, it ripped all the skin and body tissue from around his midsection but didn't tear the stomach lining. Yes, he lived, but it certainly ended his logging career.

Like I said before, good loggers were hard to find in Haines. The boss man hired a green kid to chase the landing. I could see the entire logging show from the top of the log deck. I glanced over at the chaser and saw that he was at the edge of the landing watching a turn of logs coming in.

One choker setter had gotten one log "gut hooked" which means that instead of hooking the log on the end, he had put the choker in the middle of the log. Instead of being pulled in straight, the log was what a logger calls "walking up the hill," or in other words, end over end.

In a minute or two, the log would come over the hill and smack the chaser on the head and drive him straight into the ground. I screamed, yelled, and jumped up and down trying to get the yarder engineer's attention or at least the chaser's attention.

The engineer saw me and shut down. In the meantime, the loader operator had spun around and threw the tongs. He saw I had my back turned, and slammed on the line brake just in time. The tongs clanged together just above my head.

When scared, I get mad. Down off the log deck I go, yell at and fire the kid, and send him back to town in the first log truck leaving the landing. All this, and I'm not even the boss. Someone now has two jobs, namely me.

So it's up onto the log deck, set the tongs, down the deck, and unhook the chokers over and

Log walking
up the hill

over for the rest of the day. The next morning, the boss is on the job. He tells me that I did the right thing and told me, "I'll hire the first good chaser I can find. Could you do both jobs until I find one?"

I told the owner I would try. The rest of the week goes by with no chaser. Saturday rolls around, and the boss informed me, "I can't find anyone who can handle the job. You seem to be keeping up. If I pay you wages for both jobs, will you finish out the season?"

What could I say but that I would try. I tried and did it. I went from 175 pounds to 160 pounds in a very short time, but I sure was making good money so it wasn't all that bad. That just meant that I could drop one weight class when I stopped at the good old Occidental Bar in Juneau on the way out.

It wasn't all bad as we only worked six days a week. This left Saturday night to party and Sunday to heal up. One Saturday evening after work, we were returning to town. The road ran along the Chilkoot River.

Someone spotted a bank net that the natives used to catch salmon that was threshing around right lively. The Kings were running so we knew it had to be a big salmon. Later at the bar, we started talking about having a salmon barbecue. One of the loggers had a pickup. Need I say more?

Three of us jump in the pickup and up the river we go. We got to the location of the net, stopped, and, yes, the net was still threshing. Now it's time to pick the villain to rob the net.

The pickup driver clamed he had to stay with the pickup. The other guy was overweight and slow so he volunteered to be the lookout because we knew that whatever native that owned the net sure as hell was going to be unhappy if he caught us. Who did that leave? Mr. Stupid of course.

With my usual "oh hell, why not?" down to the river I went. I grabbed the net and gave it a big pull. Mistake of course. There was a huge salmon in the net and he was a long way from being dead. The salmon responded to the pull with a jerk of his own. Into the river I went.

Now, I'm in his element and the fight is on with each of us taking turns of being on top. If you don't believe it, try wrestling a 60-pound, or bigger, King Salmon in the water. It wasn't fun, but, hell, I couldn't get any wetter or muddier, so I hung in there. Finally I got one hand in his gills and a headlock with the other arm and victory was mine.

Back to the Pioneer Bar we go to enter with the prize with me dripping wet and muddy but victorious.

Since the water was on the chilly side and the night air was about the same, I knew immediately I had to increase my alcohol level and proceeded to do just that. It probably saved my life.

I can even tell you what I was drinking, Vodka and cranberry juice. It didn't taste too good, but it sure was pretty when I upchucked. Yes, we did have the salmon barbecue the next day, but needless to say I was way too sick to enjoy it much.

Haines is where I met a man that had been mauled by a big brown bear. If I remember right, his last name was Hess, or something like that. He was a yarder engineer on the logging show I was on and was a really nice guy. His face was pushed in on one side where a person's cheekbone would be. He had a glass eye and lots of scars. He told me this story over lunch one day.

"I had a small logging show of my own. I was checking out a timber sale when I noticed a really bad smell." I couldn't help myself and asked if it was like an old dog with bad breath. He said "Yeah, about like that. How did you know?" I told him my bear story, but it turned out to be a damn weak story compared to his.

He continued on with his story. "I spun around to see what the smell was. There was this huge brown bear towering over me. When I turned, my 30-06 was pointed right at his chest. I decided not to shoot as he was already mad as hell, and I didn't want to make him any madder. The bear grabbed me by the head and clamped down hard.

"That's all I can remember about that part as I passed out for I don't know how long. When I came to, I struggled to my feet which was a big mistake. I saw the damned bear standing on a small hill about 100 yards away just watching me. Here he came in high gear, grabbed me by the shoulder, shook me like a rag doll and threw me to the ground.

"Then the son of a bitch bit me on the ass. I passed out a second time. When I came to again and started to get up once more, I saw the bear watching me from the same hill. He started back towards me once more.

"I fell to the ground and said to myself, 'please, God, no more. I've had all this fun I can stand.' I laid there quietly for what seemed like forever and finally chanced a peek to see if the bear was gone. Yes, there is a God. The bear had left.

"I don't know how I did it, but I managed to crawl a mile and a half out of the woods to the Haines Highway and collapsed on the roadway. Luckily some wonderful woman who was driving by, stopped, and helped me into her car. She hauled me to the hospital in Haines where the doctors did their best to patch me up.

"I hate to admit this, but I was still so terrified that the hospital had to let my 'old lady' come in and sleep with me as I couldn't stay alone. I still log but you can't get me in the woods. I'll go from the crummy to the yarder and that's it. I won't even go behind a bush if the call of nature catches me outside.

"That big brown bastard sure knocked all the macho out of me. My two boys went out with their dogs the next day, tracked him down, and killed him."

Now, tell me loggers aren't tough.

As long as I'm into bear stories, I may as well tell another one or two. In the Harbor Bar in Haines there is, or used to be, a bear head mounted and hanging on the wall above the bar if memory serves me correctly.

The funny part about that bear head was that the front teeth in the lower jaw were pointed outwards, not up like they should be. Of course I had to ask what the story was and this is what I was told.

It seems that two hunters were hunting goats or sheep in the wintertime, and it was cold as a whore's heart. This was when all bears were supposed to be taking their long winter nap. Down the mountain charges this huge, skinny brown bear. It seems he had just heard the dinner bell and they were it.

The first hunter in line had an automatic loading rifle. He took a bead and pulled the trigger. Nothing happened. He jacks in another shell with the same result, nothing. Meanwhile the big, big saw comes nearer and nearer. This time it was in the shape of a mean hungry bear with no Dudley DoRight to save the day.

So the other hunter had to spring into action. He shoots the bear several times, and the bear slides to a stop about 20 feet away from hunter number one. When they could breathe again, they examined the bear.

It seems someone had shot it on the point of the lover jaw with a 30.06, and the slug was still imbedded in the jaw causing the front teeth to fold forward. I'm sure this caused great gobs of pain that prevented the bear from hunting in his usual way. He couldn't put on enough fat to hibernate so he was up on the mountain chasing goats, sheep, and in this case men, anything to fill the void in his tummy.

Why wouldn't the first hunter's rifle fire? They determined that the grease in and around the firing pin was so cold that the pin wouldn't hit the shell hard enough to fire it. True or not, this is the story as told to me by the bartender, and we all know they never lie.

My former logging partner, Swede, related this bear tale to me. He told me this happened while he was logging out of Ketchikan in a fly-in logging camp. Every night a big black bear raided the camp's garbage cans, leaving a huge mess for the camp crew to clean up. Swede decided to put a stop to the raids. He had some large cherry bombs that the fishermen used to scare seals away from their nets.

Early one morning, Swede heard the bear slamming around the 50-gallon barrels the camp used as garbage cans, and slipped out of the bunkhouse. There was Mr. Bear with the garbage barrel turned over. The bear's head and shoulders were inside the barrel, with his butt facing toward Swede.

He told me his plan was to throw the cherry bomb at the bear and hit him right on the ass. He threw the bomb as hard as he could, but his aim was off. The toss was low, and it went between the bear's legs and exploded inside the barrel. All hell broke loose.

The bear apparently forgot he had a reverse gear. With his head still in the barrel, the bear ran full speed ahead, running into buildings, trees, equipment, anything and everything in his path. He finally shook loose of the barrel, crashed through the brush, and sped out of sight.

My former partner told me that, all the time this circus was going on, the bear was exercising both ends of his body at the same time, his lungs by bawling loudly and his bowels. I have heard a bear bawl. It sounds like a huge calf that's lost its mother. Of course I don't have to tell you what was coming out the other end of the bear.

Swede went on to tell me that about three weeks later, the garbage bear was seen late one evening peeking out of the brush near camp. Someone clapped his hands, and the brush snapped and crashed as Mr. Bear disappeared. I would guess it took those three weeks to rid himself of the ringing in his ears before his hearing was back to normal.

It's time now for my pathetic bear story. While working in Haines, I decided to go moose hunting. Yes, I sometimes did other things for recreation other than party. The spot I picked was next to the Porcupine River. You had to cross the river on a hand trolley suspended from a cable which was something new for me. I know I was violating every rule of safety and good sense, but why change now?

Going hunting in bear country, especially when you didn't know the countryside, is really stupid, but I did it anyway. I followed a trail through the woods for a couple of miles searching for any moose signs. I saw bear scat but ignored it and continued on my way. It was a beautiful fall day. The leaves were

109

turning color and it turned out to be more of a nature walk than a hunting trip.

I was soon to be jerked out of my dream world when a huge brown bear appeared about a hundred yards down the trail. The bear started to cross the trail, but stopped and looked up the trail at me. He didn't look like he was in any hurry so all I could do is wait to see what he would do next.

When the bear looked away for a second, I dropped to my knee and decided if he crosses the trail, fine. If he goes up the trail, great, but if he comes down the trail I'm going to start shooting and not stop until he was dead or my gun was empty. I had my 30-06 rifle loaded with seven shots of 200-grain moose slugs. If they didn't kill him, he sure would be sick as hell. If that didn't work, I would feed him the gun and run like hell.

Fortunately he made the right decision, and so did I, which was to hightail it back down the trail, across the river and head for town.

Since it's still moose season, I may as well tell my other moose story. It was about 5:00 p.m., and I was working on the high-lead show. I was on top of the log-deck and could see a long way. I saw a moose across the river. I got my rifle out of the crummy. Yes, I carried it every day as it was moose season, and we would often see them grazing along the road.

Looking through the 3x9 power scope, I could see it was a big bull. The boss was on the job that day, and I talked him into shutting down early to see if I could get the moose. Two of the loggers volunteered to go with me so down to the river we went.

First of all, we had to get across the river. Luck is with us, and we spotted a small boat tied to the bank. Seeing that nobody was around, we "borrowed" the boat and rowed across the river as quickly as possible. Using whatever cover was available, we worked our way to the swamp where the moose was feeding.

There he was standing knee deep in the swamp feeding on water plants. One shot later, our work began as we skinned the moose and cut it up in pieces small enough to haul back to camp. We knew the rest of the crew was watching, had heard the shot and could see part of the action. Now we had lots of manpower. Two of us packing the meat to the river, one ferrying it across, and the rest stowing it in the boss's pickup.

I was staying in a cheap motel so had no use for the meat, but it sure didn't go to waste. Several of the loggers were married with families living in town, including the boss. They split the meat up among them. This worked out great because most of them invited me to a moose-meat dinner more than once. The boss had the head mounted. I would guess he is still telling stories about how he bagged the giant beast.

Logging Season Over – Winter Trip South

Logging season is finally over, and it's time to head south for the winter. I boarded an Alaskan State ferry, but there is no way I can bypass Juneau without stopping. Everything is quiet in town. The Swede is working construction elsewhere. Most of the loggers have already headed south, and the fishermen are kegged up for the winter. About all that's left are the town drunks. No fun at all.

I throw my bag in the back room at the Imperial Bar and look for any excuse to stay for a day or two. The ferry would be docked in town overnight.

The rounds of all the bars are complete and still nothing. Under the circumstances, you would think I could make it out of town without getting into trouble. Wrong! Back to the Imperial Bar I go.

There at the bar with two of her friends is the biggest lady I have ever seen. Not fat, just big. She was at least two ax handles and a plug of chewing tobacco wide across the shoulders. Now illusions of grandeur set in. Of course being half shit-faced didn't hurt. I made up my mind that I was about to make my move and take out the biggest woman in Alaska. Now all I had to do is convince her.

I set the charm dial on dangerous and parked my butt on the stool next to her. I delve into chit-chat with her, and things are beginning to look good. At least she didn't knock me off the stool.

She stood up and told me, "I have to take my friend home, but I'll be back in an hour and you better still be here."

An hour gives a person a long time to think things over. I realize I'm completely out of my weight class. What would happen if we go to bed and I'm done and she isn't. Horrible scenes speed through my mind.

I have another drink, but that doesn't help. I looked at my watch and saw that half an hour had gone by. I picked up my gear, told the bartender goodbye and headed for the ferry. I still wonder what would have happened if I'd stayed and waited for her to come back to the bar.

As usual at this time of year, there were very few people on the ferry so I had my choice of where to sleep. I slept most of the first day. On the second day I wandered around the ship. It was raining and cold so I spent most of the time in the snack bar or just chatting with people. One thing about me is that you either talk, listen or just walk away.

About 6:00 p.m., the urge to have a drink took over and to the bar I go. Surprisingly there were only two people in the bar, the bartender and an attractive lady. Since I chickened out in Juneau, why not give her a go. I thought the odds were in my favor.

I could see the bartender was putting the moves on the lady, but thought about which she would prefer -- a dashing not too ugly logger or a pasty-faced lounge lizard.

It soon became obvious to even the bartender which way the lady was leaning – the right way of course. Now the lily-livered, chippy-chasing, son of a bitch of a bartender closed the bar. He told me to leave which violated every rule of fair play.

What could I do? If I thumped his melon, I would be put off the ferry at the next stop and probably be barred from riding the ferry. I graciously took the defeat, called him an asshole and went on my merry way.

I rode the ferry down to Prince Rupert so I could pick up my car at my friend Dan's place. I found out his year had been very tragic. His ten-year-old son had fallen into a hay baler operated by Dan's

113

brother. I won't go into details but needless to say his son was killed.

The next tragic event occurred when Dan ran over himself with his tractor. It didn't kill him but put him in the hospital for several weeks. Dan told me the harrowing story that he was using his tractor as a power unit for his portable sawmill.

Instead of getting up on the tractor to start it, he stood in front of the back wheel, reached over and turned the ignition key. He didn't realize that the tractor was in low gear. Before he could get away, the wheel caught his legs and ran over the full length of his body including his head.

When he fell, his head landed on a 1' x 6' board. He told me that when the tractor ran over his head, the board broke making a cracking sound. Dan thought for sure that it was his skull breaking. I don't know how he lived through the accident, as the tractor was a big Ford diesel.

He went on to tell me that he suffered and was treated for lots of broken bones, including the pelvic bone, ribs, shoulder, etc. I'm happy to say that he was up and around before I headed down to Oregon.

I ended up in Florence, Oregon, this time and rented a cabin from my mother. I went broke and ended up going to work for a contract logging outfit out of Mapleton that cut and hauled logs for a mill belonging to U. S. Plywood.

It was a low key, no hurry operation not like the gypo logging outfits I was used to working up in Alaska. They worked only eight hours a day, five days a week. Unfortunately, this left me Friday and Saturday nights to party which damn near got me killed. I didn't go steady with anyone. It was sort of catch as catch can.

It wasn't really my fault that I damn near got killed. Honest, I picked up this woman, in a bar of course, who had been living with this huge timber faller who was really tough.

When you see someone grab a good size man by the front of the shirt, wave him around like a flag, slam him against the wall leaving a big hole in the sheet rock, punching him just once putting out his lights, you know that boy is tough. She told me he had left her and went to Canada. Okay, no worries. Yah, right!

We did the town and I took her home, went in the house with her when she asked me if I wanted to spend the night. Some sixth sense kicked in, and it was saying no, no, no. I told her I was really tired and asked for a rain check. She said sure, so back to my hovel I went.

She called me the next day and reported that when she went into the bedroom and shut the door, her old boyfriend was behind it holding a baseball bat. Why he had the bat I don't know because I'm sure I couldn't even have whipped half of him on my best day.

Now you say, you were sure lucky and learned a lesson. Not! She and the huge one weren't living together anymore so I considered her fair game. Evidently he had a different opinion. The word was soon out that he was looking for me.

This sure wasn't good news for me so the honey and I didn't party in Florence but would go to the bars in Reedsport or Waldport. The only thing I had on my side was that he didn't know what I looked like, but I knew him by sight.

These evasion tactics went on for two weeks. This was the first time that I was really afraid of someone and found I couldn't live with those feelings in myself.

One Sunday morning I drove by the Fisherman's Wharf bar and saw his car. I sucked it up and walked in. Yes, he's there so I walked over to him and said, "I hear you're looking for me." His answer was "Who the hell are you?"

I responded with "I'm Larry Davis, the one you're looking for. I'm not looking for a fight, but can't live with myself by hiding and running. The fact is that common sense tells me that, in order to win in a fight with you, I would have to be lucky as hell. But I'll give it my best shot if I have to. Besides win, lose, or draw, she is the one who decides who she goes with. Hell, she probably will visit me in the hospital when this is all over."

He thought it over for a minute and said, "You're right. Besides that you've got guts. I like that. Hell, have a drink." By then, I really needed one. I bought him a drink and we parted friends.

When put in a spot like that, I'm fine while it's going on, but when I got in my car, I started shaking all over. Could have been an after effect or an adrenalin rush. The woman in question left town with the timber faller soon after that, and I sure can't say that I missed either one of them.

Since I haven't said anything crude in a while, it's time for this story. Now that romance and fear had gone from my life, I started dating a lady that worked as a cook in one of the local restaurants.

My step dad was kind of a dull shit (his own words) and loved to talk. My prudish sister had invited my Mother, dull shit, and me to dinner at their place. The conversation got around to food.

Step daddy proceeded to tell a story about the local restaurant where my current lady friend was the cook. It seems he had ordered a steak, and she went back to the cooler to get one for him. After looking the steak over, she decided it wasn't very good, put it back in the cooler and selected another one.

My step dad said "Boy, that girl sure knows a good piece of meat when she sees it." With a straight face I said, "She sure does." My brother-in-law laughed, my mother laughed, and my sister said, "You conceited bastard." All of these reactions floated over the storyteller's head.

Spring is here again and the Alaska urge is back. Time to quit my job, hit the road and head back up to Alaska.

CHAPTER VII

Return to Haines

I drove back up through Washington and British Columbia headed for Prince Rupert to see my friend Dan before I got on the ferry for Alaska. He was healed up from his encounter with the tractor.

Lo and behold, they had added a new member to their family, a baby boy. He was sort of a replacement for their son who had been killed in the hay bailer tragedy, although there is no way you can ever replace someone near and dear.

After a short visit, I boarded the ferry. There were very few people on the ferry and no trouble at all. Damn! I bypassed Juneau as my funds were low and went directly to Haines. I landed a job as landing chaser for a small gypo company that worked out of town.

As I found out last season, no matter how much money you made in town, a logger spent most of it there, including me. God, I even had to lower myself to work a winter job after my last season in Haines. I really would have preferred working at a fly-in camp to stay away from the daily temptations of town.

In spite of my in-town activities, I had a reputation as being good in the woods. Bragging maybe, but my daddy always said if you can brag without lying, it's all right to brag. A logger that I knew only by reputation had started a logging show between Haines and Juneau. When I say reputation, I mean a bad one. Supposedly he had screwed more loggers than all the native girls in Juneau. I never took a poll but am sure he would be way ahead.

This time he had a partner, Marty. Marty was an honest man who owned a restaurant, motel and bar in Haines. With the bad reputation of the logger, it was almost impossible for Marty to hire good loggers. It was next to impossible to run a logging show with greenhorns and farmers.

Marty, the bar owner, was always on my ass to go to work for their company. The offer kept getting better and better. Finally I told Marty, "If you guarantee my wages, I'll go, but if I don't get paid, I'll spend all winter in your motel, eat at your restaurant and drink at your bar." He shuddered at the thought but said, "Deal."

They flew me out to the camp. I found out that it was sort of a family affair. The owner, Wally, was a cat skinner, and his wife was chief cook and bottle washer. They had a know-it-all son-in-law who ran a 966 loader, one more cat operator and one other choker setter. I was the choker setter for Wally.

The camp was comfortable. Wally's wife was an excellent cook, as well as a very nice lady. The camp lacked a lot of creature comforts like having a two-way radio.

I think at the time not having a radio was against the law. Their only contact with the outside was to fly a big red balloon from the top of a flagpole. Whatever bush pilot who spotted the balloon would fly in and check to see what our needs were. Crude, but it worked.

I'd been in camp for only a few days when who should arrive at camp but the Swede. Once again, we caught up on old times, played cribbage, and had a lot of laughs. We had many stories to tell each other as he had wintered in Alaska with his sweetheart.

Working as a peon while your boss is running cat is never a picnic. There was Wally's way, L.D.'s way and sometimes the right way. We each had some advantages over the other. He was half owner, but he needed people like me if he was going to make money on the logging operation. Wally was bright enough to know this.

So, the war was on with neither one of us wanting to give an inch. If he wanted to take one turn of logs, I had already hooked up another. In spite of the controversies, we managed to get our share of logs to the landing.

Wally also had a hearing problem. In order to get his attention, I would throw a dirt clod or stick at the cat aiming at the screen in back of the cab. With that method of communication, the law of averages will tell you something would go wrong.

It was getting late in the year so we'd had our first snowfall. Wally was going forward with the cat but backing up was my plan. I gave a huge yell and fired a snowball at the screen in back of the cab. He turned around just as the snowball hit the screen.

As his face was just inches from the screen, it was like he took a cream pie in the face. Was he mad? Boy, he was hot. Did I think it was funny?

You bet. I'm rolling on the ground and gasping for air while laughing my ass off. He stopped the cat and lumbers off. By this time, I'm back on my feet. My thoughts were, "Am I going to have to hurt the old fool?"

He paused for a minute, thought it over and climbed back on the cat. Not a word was said. He must have told his wife about the incident because a few days later when he wasn't around, she said, "I wish I could have seen that. It sure must have been funny."

I assured her that it was. Her response was "Why do I always miss the good parts?"

All Wally's equipment was antique, except for the loader. The cats were all D-7's with cable blades and no hydraulics, but they got the job done. The other loggers all felt that I had turned out to be the camp pet. Good old Wally decided he had to go to town to order fuel and supplies.

I could see his wife was apprehensive when he got on the plane. A week goes by with no Wally, no fuel, no supplies, no nothing. Early one morning she said, "Larry, fly the balloon. You and I are going to town and get the no good son-of-a-bitch before he spends all our damn money." The next day a plane flew in to see what we needed.

On the way to town, she explained what my job would be when we got there. She continued with the instructions, "When we find the asshole, I'm going to take what money he has left to buy fuel and supplies. If he gives me any argument, knock him on his dumb ass." A dirty job, but someone had to do it. Why me though?

We flew into Juneau and his wife told me, "I know just where to find the drunken fool. Let's go to the Imperial Bar." We went to the bar just in time to see the door to the back room fly open, and there was our hero, Wally, drunk as a waltzing piss ant. He's clutching a big paper bag almost full of money, $5, $10, and $20 bills. Money is falling out of his jacket pockets.

I glanced into the back room and saw almost all the bar owners from town plus Marty, Wally's partner, from Haines. A dice box is on the table. I know now that they had been playing 4-5-6, a popular dice game up there.

Wally's wife took the paper bag and dumped the contents of bills into her purse, searched Wally's pockets and took all the money. She gave him $100 back and gave him his orders, "Go ahead and finish your drunk. Larry and I will order the supplies and fuel. Be at the flying service at 5:30 p.m. today or so help me, you're going to get your ass kicked." All this time, poor Wally is standing there just shaking his head in agreement.

We arrived at the flying service shortly before 5:30 p.m., and there was Wally passed out in a chair. We poured him into the plane and flew out to camp. We sort of helped, mostly dragged, him to the cook shack, sat him down and poured him a cup of coffee.

She rambled on saying, "Good thing we got there when we did. You don't know how many times when I caught up with him, he has blown the whole logging check."

We counted the money she had confiscated from Wally at the bar. It was over $63,000. Talk about happy, she was on "cloud nine." She thanked me profusely for going with her, and said, "Christ, Larry, you didn't even have time for a drink. Here's a $50 bonus." Sometimes even clean living pays off.

Finally the snow got too deep to log, and the season is over. Everyone except Wally, his wife and I headed for town. Wally had this plan that I would help him overhaul the engine on one of his obsolete cats.

I tried to explain that I wasn't a diesel mechanic, but to no avail. He got a gunny sack full of parts and a book on how to do the overhaul. His wife is all for anything to keep Wally out of town.

Wally would read the instruction book and give directions to me. After about a week, the job is done. Now it's time to give it a try. To my great surprise, the cat started and ran like a finely tuned watch. This success led Wally to order more parts, and we set out to overhaul the second cat.

Time sure flies fast when you are having fun. Before I knew it, the calendar told me it was December 21st, and I had to head back to Oregon so I could spend Christmas with my boys.

By now, the snow is really deep. We started one of the recently overhauled cats, pushed out a runway for the plane, flew the balloon and waited for the plane. Sure enough, a plane headed for Haines saw the balloon and landed on our freshly plowed runway. The pilot had a load of supplies, but he had room for one passenger and his gear. Me!

We loaded my stuff on the plane, taxied down the runway to turn around so we could take off into the wind. As the pilot spun the plane around, one of the wheels hit the snow berm. Suddenly the plane was standing on its nose. I was slammed against the control panel, which resulted in a black eye and the loss of a hunk of skin on one side of my face. Just what I needed.

The pilot called in on his radio for another plane. He said he also needed a mechanic, and they should bring a new propeller. An hour later, the other plane flew in. They unloaded the mechanic, tools and the new prop. Then they loaded my gear into the replacement plane, I got aboard, and we headed to Haines.

I headed for Marty's bar to pick up my check, but Wally hadn't sent all the time in yet. Marty asked me whether it would be ok if he gave me a $2,000 check with a promise to send the rest of the money when he got my time from Wally. I'm in a hurry to get back south before Christmas, so say "Hell, yes."

CHAPTER VIII

Final Trip South

I can see the fog is already settling in. I called the regular airline to see if they had a flight to Juneau that day. No way, they are fogged in. I had one more chance so I called Bennett's Air Service and got Mr. Bennett himself. I asked if he would fly me to Juneau to catch the flight to Portland. His answer was, "It's foggy as hell, but I have business to take care of in Juneau."

His next question was "Do you have $50?" I said, "You bet, in good old American cash." His next question was "Where are you?" I told him "The Pioneer Bar." He said he would pick me up in half an hour which he did.

Now the fog is really thick. Even the sea gulls are walking. We threw my gear into his Super Cub plane, and now it's Juneau here we come, I hope. We followed the Gastineau Channel all the way to Juneau flying about twenty feet above the water. Mr. Bennett is talking and cursing. He doesn't seem a bit worried, but I am. As we got close to Juneau, the fog started to lift. Maybe I'll get out of Juneau after all.

We land without incident at the Juneau airport and haul my stuff to the main terminal. Luck is still with me. A plane is scheduled to leave in two hours for Seattle with a connecting flight to Portland available. One seat was left but it was first class. I purchased the ticket, and called my baby sister in Portland. I told her my flight schedule and she said, yes, she could meet the plane.

Finally, the plane takes off with me sitting in the first class cabin. I was getting lots of funny looks from my co-passengers. Here I sit, full beard, long hair, a black eye and a huge scab on my face Not a pretty sight.

The guy seated next to me was all dressed up in his Fred Meyer suit. He kept giving me the bad eye like he expected me to jump up and mug him. His attitude soon wore me out. All I wanted to do was rest. My face hurt, my eye throbbed, and I was tired as hell.

I turned to my fine suited seat companion and told him, "I know I don't look like much, but I bet I have more Goddamn money in my pocket than you do. So stop your fucking staring at me, it's beginning to bother me. Just leave me alone." I think he looked straight ahead for the rest of the trip. I can't be sure though because I dozed off.

I arrived in Portland. There was baby sister and her brand new husband whom I had never met. She told me later that she had spotted me coming down the gangplank and told Ed, her husband, "There's my brother."

It shook him up a bit as he nervously asked, "That's your brother?" Sharon told Ed she thought so. I think he found out later that I wasn't nearly as bad as I looked. So ended my tramp logging career, but not my love affair with Alaska.

End of Tramp Logging Career

After my carefree fun-filled years as a tramp logger in Alaska, I decided to stay in Oregon. I threw away my cork boots and went back to being a sliver picker. Why, you ask? There were several reasons.

One reason was the saying that "If you survive the first year in the woods when you don't know anything, stay only until you think you know everything, then get out before you get careless and get killed."

I remarried my ex-wife and went back to work for the same lumber company I had worked for before leaving Oregon to head for Alaska. Yes, there was another reason besides stupidity that I put myself in the same marriage again. I wanted to be with my boys again.

I bailed out of the marriage when my older boy graduated from high school and left for the Naval Academy at Annapolis. The reasons were that she couldn't change, and I wouldn't change. The divorce was easier for me this time as I was the dumper, not the dumpee.

I was granted custody of my younger son who had just turned sixteen. All in all though, those years spent with my boys back in Oregon were well worth while although I never lost my love for Alaska. When the pipeline was being built in Prudhoe Bay, it was "Alaska, here I come again," but that's a story for another time.

GLOSSARY OF LOGGING TERMS

- A -

Arch　　A framework through which a winchline from a skidder passes over and is used to suspend the leading ends of logs being dragged (skidded).

Arched Skidding　　Skidding logs with an arch to raise the front of the logs off the ground as opposed to "ground skidding".

-B-

Block　　A wooden or metal case enclosing one or more pulleys used to lead a line in a specific direction, and provided with a hook, eye, or strap by which the unit may be attached to an object such as a spar tree or anchor.

Boom　　A raft of logs or a string of logs chained together, end to end, used to hold floating logs. A means of log storage or transportation.

Bull Logging Block　　Mainline lead block in high-lead logging.

Butt-Cut　　The first and largest in diameter of

130

the logs taken from a tree, directly
above the stump.

Butt- Rigging	A system of swivels and clevises which connect the haulback and mainline together and to which butt hooks are fastened. An essential part of high-lead cable logging system. The heavy metal knobs and rings, suspended from the mainline, to which chokers are attached.

- C -

Calks	The logger's steel-spiked, high boots which gives him steady footing on logs. For some reason, always called "corks".
Cat	Bulldozer
Cat Logging	(Ground skidding) Pulling logs parallel to the ground with or without using an arch to raise the front end of the logs.
Cat Skinner	One who operates a cat.
Chaser	The person who unhooks the chokers from the logs at the landing.
Choker	A small length of cable, equipped with a knob and bell, put around logs to

131

yard them in. A nubbin on the end fits into a sliding bell on the cable so when pulled, cinches up tight and attaches the logs to the butt-rigging of cable systems, or to tractor skidders. Chokermen (choker setters) say a choker is an instrument of torture invented by people who hate loggers.

Choker Setter — Also "chokerman". A person who attaches chokers to logs. Usually the first (and toughest) job a logger gets.

Cold-Deck — (Log Deck) A pile of stored logs which will be moved at some future date.

Crummy — A logger's bus.

Cull — Applied to a log, it means a useless, rotten log. Applied to a person, it means pretty much the same thing. A logger's strong insult.

- D -

Donkey — Logging machine

Donkey Doctor — Mechanic

Donkey Puncher	The man who runs the heavy diesel powered yarders and loaders. The name is a relic from the old days of steam.
Drum	A spool around which a cable is wound.

- E -

Eye	A loop at the end of a wire rope secured by splicing or press fitted.

- F -

Faller	A logger who actually cuts down the tree. Also called cutter, chopper, busheler.

- G -

Guy Lines	Wire rope lines from a yarding machine to substantial anchors for support against yarding forces, lines to hold a spar tree steady.
Grapple	A heavy set of hinged metal tongs with teeth on the inside edge, which can be opened and shut at will by the yarder operator.

Grapple Show	A method of logging in which a grapple, rather than a choker, is used to haul in logs.
Gypo	(Also known as a Busheler) Logger/contractor who works at piece rates. Usually used to refer to independent loggers vs. company-hired loggers.

- H -

Haulback	A cable which is used to pull the mainline with butt rigging, with chokers, back to the timber for the next turn at the worksite.
Haulback Block	A block in a cable yarding system used to guide the haulback line. In some systems, may also be called a tailback.
Haywire	The essential baling wire that keeps so many operations going. Also, an adjective meaning "patched up" or "no good." Sometimes used to describe a light cable used to pull a heavier cable.
High-Lead Logging	A cable system of logging best used for uphill and/or rough terrain. Lead blocks are hung on a spar tree to provide lift to the font end of the logs. The lower main line is used for the skidding line. The upper secondary

line is looped out around the woods with several blocks on the back side of the job. As the area is logged the blocks are disconnected one at a time, causing the main line to realign itself with the next tail block, thus changing roads.

A spar tree (a tall, centrally located tree that is topped, rigged with blocks and guy lines and used as a derrick for yarding in trees from the area being logged) -- The spar tree is the center of the cable system setup which is where the main line, the haulback line and the chokers all come together by use of butt rigging. It is essentially a ground logging system in that the logs normally drag on the ground on their way to the landing. It is called high-lead because the main line is elevated and this assists the logs in riding over obstacles.

In many ways, the high-lead system is simply two winch lines. One to drag logs in to the machine and a second to drag the winch line back out into the woods. The rigging is simple and only a two-drum machine is required and is best used for uphill logging. (See sketch below of a high-lead cable system configuration.)

135

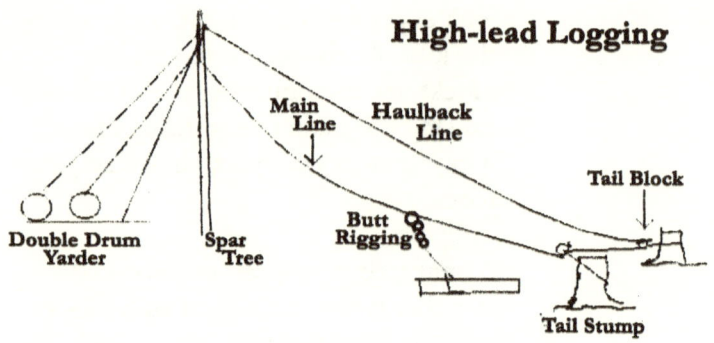

High-lead Logging

Main Line · Haulback Line · Tail Block · Double Drum Yarder · Spar Tree · Butt Rigging · Tail Stump

Hook Tender	Boss of the rigging crew

- L -

Landing	A place to which logs are dragged for loading.
Logging Show	A logging operation.

- M -

Mainline	The heavy cable which is wound up on the drums of the yarder and which drags the logs to the landing.
"Make 'er Out"	"Spill the ink." / "Make out the check, I quit!"

Nosebag   A portable lunch-bucket.

Peavey   A steel spiked pole with a hinged tong,
               which provides the leverage necessary
               for moving large logs.

Rigging   Anyone who is a member of the crew
Crew   that handles or works on cables.

Rigging   One who spots chokers over logs.
Slinger

Road   Moving to an area adjacent to a
Change   cleaned up logging site. Done by
               the tail-hold.

Side   A logging operation, but more
               specifically, the place where it is going
               on. Thus a "logging show"
               (operation) could have one or more
               sides.

Siwash   A line not running in a straight line by
               being bent around a tree, stump, rock,
               etc.

Skidder	A self-propelled machine, either tracked or rubber-tired, used to drag logs to the landing.
Slash	Debris left after a logging operation.
Spar-Tree	A tall, centrally located tree that is topped, rigged with blocks and guy lines and used as a derrick for yarding in trees from the area being logged.
Spike-Table	A table of food where the logger can make up his own menu, usually for his nosebag. (bagged lunch)
Spotter	A man equipped with a walkie-talkie radio, who directs the yarder operator on a grapple show.
Strap	Short piece of line for a block.
Straw-Line	A small light cable, usually 3/8" or less in diameter, used to string heavier line.

- T -

Tailblock	A block at the back end of the yarding area which is used to guide the haulback line and is attached to an anchored spar tree.

Tailhold	A sturdy stump or tree which is used to support a block through which cable runs back to the yarder.
Talkie Tooter	A portable radio transmitter, carried by one of the choker setters or rigging slinger on a cable operation, which operates a whistle on the yarder and signals the yarder engineer which cable maneuvers to initiate. Talkie Tooter is a brand name for the most commonly used make of these radio controlled systems and is often used generically, much like Kleenex or Coke, in woods conversations. Also a "bug".
Tie Back	A line attached to a secondary stump from the main anchor stump to distribute the load on the anchor. Commonly used where one log stump is not available to provide adequate anchorage.
Timber Beast	A logger, especially a rough, crude one.
Tongs	Pair of curved arms with sharp points pivoted like scissors to bite into a log for yarding or loading.
Trip Line	Haulback line

Turn	A load of logs, especially as it refers to skidder or yarder equipment.

- W -

Wanigan	A floating cook-house and bunkhouse used as a home by the crew members of a log-drive.
Whistle-Punk	The man who actuated the whistle of an old-time yarder by pulling on a light wire. A somewhat archaic term for the person who controls the whistle now mostly done by radio.
Widow Maker	A loose limb barely hanging on a tree. It seems to always fall on a logger.
Winch	A powered drum at the back of a cat used to reel in or pay out cable for yarding or hoisting.

Yarder	A machine or system of winches used to haul logs into a landing. Technically it is just the power and winch system of the machine that powers the mainline.
Yarder Engineer	Person who operates and is responsible for the yarder.
Yarding	The act or process of conveying logs to a landing. In common practice, yarding is often reserved for cable logging, while skidding is used for ground level logging.